Lovestories 4 Girls

# Kisses in the Snow

Julia Ross



Compact Verlag

**Bisher sind in dieser Reihe erschienen:**

Band 1: Full Moon Kisses
Band 2: Last Chance for a First Date
Band 3: Flirt But Don't Fall in Love
Band 4: Trouble in Seventh Heaven
Band 5: Heartbreak Summer
Band 6: First Love on a Rainy Day
Band 7: Kisses in the Snow
Band 8: Love Changes All
Band 9: No Risk, No Love
Band 10: Kick-off for Love

**Weitere Titel sind in Vorbereitung.**


Chefredaktion: Dr. Angela Sendlinger
Redaktion: Helga Aichele
Fachredaktion: Oliver Astley
Produktion: Wolfram Friedrich
Illustrationen: Bettina Weisl (MA Illustration)
Typografischer Entwurf: textum GmbH
Umschlaggestaltung: Bettina Weisl (MA Illustration)

ISBN: 978-3-8174-7880-4
7278801

Besuche uns im Internet: www.compactverlag.de

# Vorwort

Mit dieser spannenden und romantischen Compact Lovestory kannst du deine Englischkenntnisse spielend leicht verbessern. Eine deutsche Einleitung vor jedem neuen Kapitel hilft dir, den englischen Text zu verstehen. Außerdem werden auf jeder Seite die etwas schwierigeren Wörter erklärt, und durch die Zeichnungen bekommst du eine genauere Vorstellung von den vier Girls und ihren aufregenden Erlebnissen. Blätter doch einfach mal durch!

Jedes Kapitel wird durch Übungen und Tests ergänzt, die richtig spannend und abwechslungsreich sind: Da geht es um Jungs und Liebe, Partys, Freundschaft und Mode – so wird Englischlernen richtig spannend und cool!

Die Antworten und Lösungen kannst du gleich ins Buch schreiben und hinterher im Lösungsteil nachlesen, ob du alles richtig gemacht hast und was die Tests über dich aussagen. Und wenn du möchtest, kannst du alle Vokabeln im Glossar noch einmal nachschlagen. Slang-Ausdrücke sind mit einem ϟ gekennzeichnet.

Wir wünschen dir viel Spaß mit Holly und ihren Freundinnen – und natürlich viel Erfolg beim Englischlernen!

# Inhalt

1

# Snowed In

# 1

Am Montagmorgen wird die verschlafene Holly von ihrem Vater mit einer guten Nachricht geweckt: Es hat stark geschneit und deshalb fällt die Schule aus. Holly bestaunt gerade ihren verschneiten Garten, als sie plötzlich einen Schneeball abbekommt. Daniel! Nach einer ordentlichen Schneeballschlacht genießen die beiden den schulfreien Tag.
Am nächsten Abend kochen sie zusammen, als Holly siedend heiß einfällt, dass sie ja eigentlich mit ihren Freundinnen zum Feuerwerk verabredet ist! Sie kommt gerade noch rechtzeitig …

Holly yawned and pulled the quilt back up over her face. It was a Monday morning, but the thought of school soon disappeared from her mind as she slowly drifted back to sleep. Her body felt heavy in the warm bed and her eyes refused to open. Suddenly, she heard her father's voice. He normally left the house for work before Holly woke up, but this morning she was too tired to find the sound unusual.

| | |
|---|---|
| to yawn | gähnen |
| quilt | Bettdecke |
| to drift | gleiten, ziehen |
| to refuse | sich weigern, ablehnen |

The voice got louder. "Holly! Wake up!"

Holly rolled over and pulled the quilt further up, so that now only her brown hair could be seen beneath it.

| | |
|---|---|
| to spill | strömen; verschütten |
| to adjust (to) | sich gewöhnen an, sich anpassen |
| scene | Aussicht, Szenerie |
| to line | säumen (Straße) |
| buried | *hier:* verschneit |

"Look, Holly," said her father, who was now beside the window. He opened the curtain and let the light spill into the room.

Holly yawned again, more loudly this time. Finally, she opened her eyes and waited for them to adjust to the light. Now she began to realize: yes, there *was* something unusual about this morning. Her eyes did not seem to be adjusting – everything still looked so bright outside.

"We're snowed in!" said her father happily. "You can't go to school today, I'm afraid – I hope you aren't too disappointed!"

Holly quickly sat up and looked through the window at the beautiful scene. Snow covered the garden and lay like a thick blanket on top of the cars that lined the buried street outside.

"Wait a minute, Dad," she said. "Why aren't you at work?"

"Even dads get snowed in," he replied with a smile. "Have you seen the road out there? It wouldn't be safe for me to drive to work today."

He switched on Holly's television and the screen filled with more winter scenes. The news presenter seemed to agree with Holly's father. She explained that many roads were not safe and that nobody should drive anywhere unless they really had to.

"What about the train?" Holly asked.

But before the words had left her mouth, new pictures had appeared on the television. First they showed an empty train station covered in snow, then a picture of a departure board at the station. The presenter read the words that were written on it: "All trains are cancelled."

| | |
|---|---|
| screen | Bildschirm |
| news presenter | Nachrichten-sprecher |
| departure board | Abfahrts-anzeige |
| to be cancelled | gestrichen sein |
| to join sb. | sich zu jmd. gesellen |

Outside, the snow was still falling lightly.

Holly did not feel tired any-more. She jumped out of bed and pulled on her coat with-out even changing out of her brightly coloured pyjamas. Then she put on a large, red hat and some warm shoes before running to the door and walking out into the pure white landscape.

"It's so beautiful!" she shouted as her father hurried to join her.

He looked just as excited as she was. Inside the house, Holly's mum smiled at the two of them from behind the living room window.

"Look at this!" Holly's dad said, pointing at a tree in their garden. It looked like a sculpture with its dark branches covered in thick fingers of snow.

Holly looked around at the other trees and plants before her eyes came to rest on the family car. Its wheels were buried and the windows were completely covered.

"I'm not surprised you didn't want to drive to work today!" she said. "Such a lot of snow!"

Suddenly, she felt something hard hit her arm. She looked down in surprise and saw white powder spill down her coat.

"Dad!" she shouted.

Her father turned around with a surprised look on his face and asked her what had happened.

| | |
|---|---|
| sculpture | Skulptur |
| branch | Zweig |
| powder | Pulver, Puder |
| to wipe | (ab)wischen |
| to surrender | aufgeben, sich ergeben |

Holly did not have long to wonder who had thrown the snowball before another one hit her in the face. As she wiped the snow from her eyes, she saw someone move behind the car. Without thinking, she took some snow from the roof of the car and made it into a tight ball with her hands. She slowly moved around the car and threw the snowball as hard as she could at whoever was hiding there. She watched it break into powder all over a boy in a blue coat.

"I surrender!" he laughed.

Even covered in snow, Holly recognized him immediately: it was Daniel, her boyfriend.
Holly gave him a mischievous smile and started to make another snowball as she walked closer. Daniel put one hand over his face as though he was trying to protect himself. But then, suddenly, he threw another snowball at her. He had been hiding it behind his back the whole time.

Holly screamed happily and threw her own snowball at Daniel. Soon they were both running around, throwing snow at each other and hiding behind the cars. Finally, they both fell onto the thick blanket of snow in the garden and started laughing.

| | |
|---|---|
| mischievous | verschmitzt |
| pattern | Muster |
| fluffy | flauschig |
| slippers | Hausschuhe |
| to suppose | denken, anehmen |
| to giggle | kichern |
| to aim | zielen |

"Look what you've done to my pyjamas!" said Holly in between laughter.

Daniel rolled over to look at her. Her coat had fallen open to show the pattern of colourful stars on her pyjamas. He laughed even harder when he noticed the strange outfit under her warm winter coat.

"Me and you were made for each other," he said and pointed at his feet.

Holly looked downwards. He was wearing bright, fluffy slippers.

"I suppose we were!" she giggled, before moving closer to kiss him.

The warmth of his lips took her by surprise and made her suddenly notice how cold the morning was.

"Come on, let's go inside," she said.

"Wait, I want to remember this moment."

Daniel took a digital camera from his coat pocket, held it out in his hand and aimed it at the two of them from above. After taking the picture, he showed it to Holly. Their own happy faces smiled back at them on the camera screen.

| | |
|---|---|
| to exclaim | ausrufen |
| to get one's priorities right | seine Prioritäten (richtig) setzen |

"What a great picture!" Holly exclaimed. "But wait a minute. You didn't have time to put on shoes and yet you managed to bring a camera?!"

"Of course," replied Daniel. "You have to get your priorities right, you know."

***ÜBUNG 1:** Hidden words. Finde im Suchrätsel neun Wörter aus dem Text!*

| | | | | | | | | | | |
|---|---|---|---|---|---|---|---|---|---|---|
| X | A | P | Y | J | A | M | A | S | Y | L |
| B | S | P | A | H | R | E | T | B | U | P |
| V | N | A | W | E | S | P | D | S | E | G |
| E | O | M | N | I | C | O | A | T | J | I |
| N | W | T | O | N | F | W | B | E | Z | G |
| A | B | G | P | W | A | D | G | M | O | G |
| T | A | W | M | I | Z | E | V | R | F | L |
| S | L | I | P | P | E | R | S | I | J | E |
| H | L | U | B | E | X | U | C | H | O | Z |
| I | M | F | A | Z | L | K | I | X | S | A |
| K | J | E | M | W | I | N | D | O | W | U |

Holly and Daniel lived in the same street, so it was easy for them to see each other whenever they wanted to – which was almost all the time. Holly felt like they had spent all of the last weeks together, ever since they had started going out. They even walked to school together every morning.

So that day, seeing Daniel so early in the morning was nothing unusual. Daniel had to go home to change his shoes, but before Holly could feel bored without him he came back over to her house.

| | |
|---|---|
| to chat | plaudern |
| to interrupt | unterbrechen |
| absentmindedly | geistesabwesend |
| curly | lockig |

The hours started to drift away while the two of them chatted. Even when they were watching a DVD, they talked so much that neither of them really knew what was happening in the film.

Their conversation only stopped when they were interrupted by the sound of the telephone ringing.

Holly picked up the phone.

"Hello."

"Hi, Hol, it's me," said a familiar voice.

It was her German friend, Nina.

"Oh, hi, Nina," Holly said absentmindedly.

With her left hand she was playing with Daniel's curly hair. "Are you enjoying the day off?"

"Yeah, of course," Nina replied. "But I can't believe that everything is closed just because of some snow! Are you watching the news? The whole country has stopped working!"

Holly looked back at the romantic film on her television screen.
"Yeah, I guess so," she said as Daniel put his arm around her. She smiled at him.
"I'm just worried that Bonfire Night will be cancelled, too," Nina added.
Suddenly, Holly remembered that she and her two other best friends had promised to go to the celebrations with Nina. They had decided not to invite any boys along, so for once Holly had agreed to spend an evening without Daniel.
Before coming to England, Nina had never heard of Bonfire Night. She was interested in finding out more about the country's traditions and wanted to see this one for herself.

| | |
|---|---|
| Bonfire Night | Die Nacht des 5. November, zur Erinnerung an den 1605 gescheiterten Plan, das Parlament zu sprengen |
| to promise | versprechen |
| celebration | Feier |
| firework display | Feuerwerk |
| to sigh | seufzen |

"Oh, I'd forgotten that was tomorrow night," said Holly. "Hopefully the snow will have stopped by then. It looks like it's getting lighter, so we might be lucky."
"I hope so," Nina said. "I've really been looking forward to it."
Luckily, Bonfire Night was not cancelled the next day in spite of the heavy carpet

of snow that still lay over the town. It was six o'clock and Evie and Emily had already come to meet Nina in time for the firework display at half past six. But none of them knew where Holly was.

"Have you tried calling her?" asked Evie impatiently. "We should go soon."

"I've called her three times," Nina sighed. "But you're right. Actually, we should leave now."

*ÜBUNG 2: True or false? Kreuze die richtigen Aussagen an!*

1. Holly and Daniel saw each other most mornings. ❑
2. Daniel was wearing fluffy slippers instead of shoes in the garden. ❑
3. Holly paid close attention to the film that she was watching. ❑
4. Nina had never heard of Bonfire Night in Germany. ❑
5. The snow was not a problem for most of the country. ❑
6. Holly's mother came to wake her up. ❑
7. Holly was only partly paying attention to her conversation with Nina. ❑

| | |
|---|---|
| to advise | (be)raten |
| to trudge | trotten, latschen |
| wellington boots | Gummistiefel |
| contest | Wettbewerb |
| passion | Leidenschaft |

The three girls walked out into the cold night together in their warmest winter clothes. The celebrations were taking place in a large field next to the school, so Evie and Emily had advised Nina to dress very warmly. Now, as Nina trudged through the snow in her green wellington boots, she was glad that they had told her to wear three pairs of socks.

"I can't believe Holly forgot," said Emily.

Evie let out a short, sharp laugh. "I can! She must be with Dan again, and when she's with him she forgets about everything else. The sky could turn bright green and she'd be too lost in her romantic daydreams to notice."

"She's always been like that, I suppose," Emily added.

It was true that Holly had never seemed very interested in the real world. She preferred daydreams to her studies, and fantasies of love to real life.

"I miss her, though," Nina said simply.

The other girls quietly agreed and carried on walking.

Holly had known Daniel since they were very young, but she had only realized that she had feelings for him when a school talent contest brought them closer together. Daniel, who was half Brazilian, had helped to teach Holly to dance the samba. Since then it had become her passion.

*ÜBUNG 3: Do you put boys before friends? Sind dir Jungs wichtiger als deine Freundinnen?*

1. A boy asks you out on a date, but you already have plans with your best friends. What do you do?
   a) ❑ Tell him you already have other plans. *(10 points)*
   b) ❑ Tell your friends you're ill and go on the date instead. *(0 points)*
   c) ❑ Ask your friends if you can meet another time. *(6 points)*

2. A boy you like asks you to dance at the school disco... but he is your friend's ex-boyfriend. Do you:
   a) ❑ Ask your friend first. *(5 points)*
   b) ❑ Dance with him and hope for a romantic kiss. *(0 points)*
   c) ❑ Say no – you don't want to hurt your friend. *(9 points)*

3. Your friends are upset because you spend a lot of time with your new boyfriend. Do you:
   a) ❑ Ignore them – they're just jealous. *(0 points)*
   b) ❑ Ask your boyfriend's opinion. *(5 points)*
   c) ❑ Make more time to see your friends. *(10 points)*

Your score: ...............

That evening, they were cooking dinner together at Daniel's house. The sound of samba wafted across the kitchen, where it met with the exotic smell of the food. Holly could not help but move her feet to the music. Daniel started to move in time with her, and, laughing, they began to dance together.

Before long the delicious aroma that had filled the room slowly turned to a smell of burning. Holly noticed the smell, stopped dancing and ran to take the food away from the heat. Then she saw a sudden flash of orange light up the sky through the kitchen window.

"Oh no! I completely forgot!" she exclaimed.

Daniel looked at her in confusion. "You completely forgot what?"

"Bonfire Night, of course!" she said, as more brightly coloured fireworks exploded outside. "I promised Nina I would go with her!"

"You should hurry then," said Daniel. "I think you can still get there in time for some of the fireworks if you run. Quick, here's your coat." He helped Holly get ready and then kissed her goodbye before she ran out of the door and down the road. Brightly coloured sparks lit up the sky all around her.

| | |
|---|---|
| to waft | wehen, tönen |
| in time | *hier:* im Takt, im Rhythmus |
| sudden | plötzlich |
| flash | Aufleuchten, Lichtblitz |
| fireworks | Feuerwerk, Feuerwerkskörper |
| spark | Funke |
| giant | riesig |
| to melt | sich auflösen, schmelzen |

Meanwhile, Nina was watching the fireworks with the other girls. Giant flashes of orange, pink and green sparks exploded above them before melting into the night sky.

*ÜBUNG 4: Prepositions. Unterstreiche die richtige Präposition!*

1. Part of Daniel's family was of/from Brazil.
2. There was a delicious smell in/on the kitchen.
3. Holly saw fireworks through/between a window.
4. Holly had forgotten of/about Bonfire Night.
5. Holly moved her feet at/to the music.
6. Daniel moved in/by time with her.
7. Daniel looked at Holly with/in confusion.
8. The sky was lit up/down by colourful sparks.
9. They were cooking dinner at/in Daniel's house.
10. The girls walked out to/into the cold night.

"So, tell me again, you do this every year because of a man called, uh... Guy Forks?" she asked the others.
"That's right, Guy Fawkes," replied Emily.

"Hundreds of years ago, he put gunpowder under the Houses of Parliament to kill the king."

"And we remember it every year by exploding things, too, except now we use fireworks instead of gunpowder," continued Evie. "Some people go to displays like this, but others just have fireworks in their gardens. And then afterwards there's always a bonfire."

"That's because Guy was burnt in a sort of bonfire himself. That's how they punished people in those days," Emily explained.

"We'll go over and look when they light the bonfire," added Evie. "You'll see them burn a model of a man on it. The model can be made out of all sorts of things, like wood and straw, and it's usually dressed in historical clothes. That's Guy."

| | |
|---|---|
| gunpowder | Schießpulver |
| Houses of Parliament | Parlamentsgebäude in London |
| bonfire | Scheiterhaufen, großes Lagerfeuer |
| to punish | bestrafen |
| straw | Stroh |
| eventually | schließlich |

"Strange," said Nina. "I understand the fireworks and the bonfire... but why do English people want to celebrate the day that someone tried to kill the king?"

Evie and Emily looked at each other and thought about it.

"Um... I really have no idea!" answered Emily eventually.

Evie was still thinking about Nina's question when she felt a hand on her arm. She turned around and saw Holly, who was out of breath, but she looked happy.

"I'm so sorry I'm late," Holly said. "But I'm here now!"

As she spoke, the last of the fireworks melted away in the sky above the girls' heads.

"It's okay," said Nina, but her expression had changed since Holly arrived. She now looked more disappointed than excited.

"No, it isn't," said Holly. "I promised to come and then I... I just forgot all about it. I was with –"

"Daniel," Evie finished Holly's sentence for her.

Holly looked away shyly. "Sorry," she said again. "We were... well... I just forgot."

Her cheeks had gone a little red.

"Well, the important thing is that you came in the end," said Nina. "Why don't we all go and watch the bonfire being lit?"

"Yeah. Let's go," Emily said enthusiastically.

The girls all moved towards the bonfire. It was huge! And just as Evie and Emily had described, there was a model of Guy Fawkes staring down from the top of it. He had a horrible grin, but Nina still felt almost sorry for him. It seemed a slightly cruel tradition to celebrate a man being burnt alive in a giant fire. However, when she looked around, the crowd did not seem cruel at all. Groups of friends were laughing and chatting together, and small children were running around in warm hats and wellington boots.

| | |
|---|---|
| cheek | Wange |
| to stare | starren |
| horrible | schrecklich |
| grin | Grinsen |
| cruel | grausam, gemein |
| crowd | (Menschen-) Menge |

*ÜBUNG 5: Reading comprehension. Beantworte die Fragen zum Text!*

1. How did Guy Fawkes try to kill the King of England?

   ..........................................................

   ..........................................................

2. How was he punished?

   ..........................................................

3. What do people do today to remember him?

   ..........................................................

   ..........................................................

4. Why was Holly late to the fireworks display?

   ..........................................................

   ..........................................................

5. What does Nina not understand about the celebrations?

   ..........................................................

   ..........................................................

6. What is the model of Guy made out of?

   ..........................................................

While the girls were waiting for the bonfire to be lit, Holly had an idea to help make it up to her friends. She went to buy something and returned as quickly as she could to show the other girls.

"Wow, sparklers!" said Emily. "I love these!"

They lit the sparklers so that bright, silver sparks flew from the ends. By moving them around quickly, they made shapes and patterns in the darkness.

"This is so much fun!" Nina exclaimed. "Look, I'm writing my name!"

The others watched as, for a second, the shapes of the letters appeared in front of her.

| | |
|---|---|
| to make it up to sb. | bei jmd. etw. wiedergutmachen |
| sparkler | Wunderkerze |
| excitement | Aufregung, Freude |

"And I'm making a heart shape!" said Holly.

"What a surprise!" joked Evie.

Their laughter was interrupted by a shout of excitement.

"Look, they're lighting the bonfire!" said a little boy next to them.

The fire quickly grew. Soon the model of Guy Fawkes was burning brightly, too.

Nina turned around to look at her friends. They were all looking at the bonfire and she could see the reflection of the fire in their eyes.

"I still think this is a strange celebration, but I'm really enjoying it," she said.

"Me too," agreed Holly. "And I'm so sorry about before."

Nina, Evie and Emily accepted her apology, but they were not so sure that anything would change. Holly was already pulling her mobile phone from her pocket, ready to call Daniel.

| | |
|---|---|
| apology | Entschuldigung |

*ÜBUNG 6: Odd one out. Welches Wort ist das „schwarze Schaf"?*

1. coat, bonfire, hat, scarf
2. ball, circle, square, triangle
3. snow, snowball, sparks, snowflakes
4. burn, light up, fire, ice
5. fireworks, bonfire, slippers, sparkler

2

# Kisses and Lies

# 2

In der Schule ist Holly wie üblich in ihren Tagträumen versunken. Nach Schulschluss stellt Daniel ihr Ivy vor, die neu in seine Klasse gekommen ist. Ivy ist Holly sofort unsympathisch. Sie würde die Zeit lieber alleine mit Daniel verbringen, anstatt Ivy überallhin mitzuschleppen. Als sie dann ein paar Tage später auf der Mädchentoilette zufällig mit anhört, dass Ivy Daniel für einen tollen Küsser hält, kann es Holly kaum fassen: Betrügt Daniel sie mit Ivy? Holly ist am Boden zerstört und will seinen faulen Ausreden nicht länger glauben …

Holly was looking down at the page in front of her, but her eyes did not focus on the words. She heard the teacher only dully, as if he was talking in a language that she did not understand.

"Psst!" said Evie, who was sitting next to her. "Do you want to go shopping after school?"

Holly awoke from her daydream and looked up from the book on her table.

"Uh... I can't. I'm seeing Dan tonight," she replied in a whisper.

Evie was not surprised. She was getting used to hearing the same words every time she invited Holly to do something.

"Fine, never mind," Evie said.

She gave a little sigh and returned to her work. The thin, grey-haired teacher continued his monologue, "...and so you can see that plants need water for photosynthesis..."

Holly looked out of the window and let her mind drift back to other thoughts. Instead of photosynthesis, she thought about an imaginary date with her boyfriend. It always made the time pass much more quickly than when she tried to listen to the boring things that her teacher talked about.

| | |
|---|---|
| to focus on | sich konzentrieren auf |
| dully | gedämpft, dumpf |
| whisper | Flüstern |
| photosynthesis | Fotosynthese |
| imaginary | imaginär, vorgestellt |
| candlelit dinner | Abendessen bei Kerzenschein |
| suit | Anzug |
| to shimmer | schimmern, schillern |
| to shatter | zerstören |

In the daydream, she and Daniel were having a romantic, candlelit dinner by a beach at sunset. He was dressed in a black suit and she was wearing a beautiful, silver dress that shimmered like the sea. Daniel leant towards her and she closed her eyes, hearing nothing but the waves. Their lips were about to touch...

Suddenly, the sound of the school bell shattered the image.

Holly put away her things and went to meet Daniel. Her friends did not wait for her like they used to – instead they walked off without her towards the shops in the town centre.

| | |
|---|---|
| to live out sth. | etw. verwirklichen, ausleben |
| to bounce with excitement | vor Aufregung hüpfen |
| glossy | glänzend |

Holly did not really notice the change in them. The only thing that she could think about was seeing Daniel and living out her romantic daydreams for real. Holly bounced with excitement as she walked towards the school gates and saw him waiting for her.

*ÜBUNG 7: Adjectives. Ergänze die fehlenden Steigerungsformen!*

| | | |
|---|---|---|
| 1. dull | .................... | dullest |
| 2. beautiful | .................... | .................... |
| 3. .................... | .................... | most romantic |
| 4. .................... | happier | .................... |
| 5. good | .................... | .................... |
| 6. .................... | worse | .................... |

With a head full of happy thoughts, Holly walked towards Daniel. But when she reached the gates, she saw that he was not alone today. Next to him was a thin girl, who was very pretty. The girl had long, glossy black hair. She looked quite childlike, even though she was wearing trendy shoes and had shortened the skirt of her school uniform. Holly disliked her immediately.

"Holly!" Daniel shouted. He smiled and called her over. "This is Ivy."

| | |
|---|---|
| sense of direction | Orientierungs-sinn |
| barely | kaum |
| gratefully | dankbar |
| to cringe | zusammenzucken, erschaudern |

"Hi, Ivy," said Holly, trying to smile. Only half of her mouth managed to turn upwards.

"Nice to meet you, Holly," said Ivy brightly. Unlike Holly, her face was lit up by a friendly grin. "Daniel's been telling me all about you."

"Ivy's the new girl in my class," explained Daniel. "Today's her first day and the teacher has asked me to show her around... you know, just until she gets to know where everything is."

"Oh right," said Holly.

At least that meant that Daniel had not chosen to spend time with this girl, she thought. Hopefully Ivy would go away once she found her own friends.

"She doesn't live very far away from us, so I thought we could help her find her way home," Daniel continued.

"Oh, that would be great," Ivy said. "I've got such a bad sense of direction. I can barely find my way out of my own front door!"

She giggled and looked at Holly and Daniel gratefully.

Holly cringed, but said nothing. She knew that Daniel was a kind person who liked helping people – she only hoped that he did not invite this Ivy girl on their date that night as well.

"So, you're new to the school then?" Holly asked Ivy as they walked.

But instead of listening to Ivy's reply, she watched Daniel's reaction closely. He was smiling at the new girl encouragingly, which made Holly shudder with jealousy.

"Yeah, my family has just moved here from London," Ivy said.

"Do you like it here?" asked Holly, without interest.

"Yes, but everything seems so small... There's not that much to do around here, is there?"

| | |
|---|---|
| closely | *hier:* genau |
| encouragingly | ermutigend |
| to shudder | zittern, erschaudern |
| jealousy | Eifersucht |
| to feel insulted | beleidigt sein |
| to bet | wetten |

Holly finally looked away from Daniel in surprise. She felt insulted by Ivy's words. Her town might not be as big as London, but she and her friends enjoyed doing plenty of things there, like shopping, going to the cinema and ice-skating. And unlike in London, you only had to travel a short distance out of town to find many beautiful, natural landscapes where you could go camping or even rock-climbing.

"It depends what you like to do," Daniel said quickly.

Luckily he had spoken before Holly, who probably would not have been so polite.

"I suppose so," said Ivy. "Anyway, do you have many parties here? I bet they're pretty crazy out here in the wilderness!"

"The wilderness?!" said Holly out loud in surprise.

Daniel looked at her sharply to let her know that she was being rude. Holly fumed silently and stared back at him while he answered Ivy's question. After what seemed like a much longer walk than normal, they finally arrived at Holly's house. Daniel explained to Ivy how she could get home and then went inside with Holly. They were going to go to the cinema that afternoon to watch an action film together. Daniel started talking about how much he was looking forward to it, but Holly was not listening.

"I can't believe she thinks we live in the wilderness!" she said, all of a sudden.

"Who?" Daniel asked absentmindedly. Then he remembered. "Oh yeah, her."

"Who does she think she is? Just because she comes from a big city doesn't make us country bumpkins who sit around watching the cows eat grass all day! I think there's plenty to do around here..."

Daniel put his hand on Holly's shoulder. "Never mind, Hol. I'm sure she didn't mean to upset you. I think she just misses London."

The touch of Daniel's hand was enough to make Holly feel much calmer. She decided to forget about what was upsetting her and enjoy her date instead. And anyway, she thought, soon Ivy would make friends and not need to spend time with the two of them anymore.

| | |
|---|---|
| to fume | schäumen (vor Wut) |
| all of a sudden | ganz plötzlich |
| ϟ country bumpkin | Landei |
| to upset sb. | jmd. aufregen |
| awkward | unangenehm |

*Übung 8: Unscramble the words. Ordne die Buchstaben in Klammern zu sinnvollen Wörtern!*

1. Holly feels *(telsinud)* .................. because Ivy thinks there is not much to do in her hometown.
2. Holly is *(soulaje)* .................. because Daniel is nice to Ivy.
3. Ivy has upset Holly, who *(sufem)* .................. silently.
4. Ivy has recently *(dovem)* .................. there from London.
5. Holly *(silidsek)* .................. Ivy immediately.
6. Holly likes to *(demarady)* .......................... .

But Holly was wrong. Ivy walked home with her and Daniel every day that week. She tried as hard as she could to be nice to Holly, but it did not seem to help.
The awkward walks home were even starting to create problems in Holly and Daniel's relationship. They normally agreed on almost everything, so they hardly ever argued. But now, Daniel could no longer stay quiet about Holly's rude behaviour.

One day, after Holly had been particularly cold and unfriendly towards Ivy, Daniel waited until they were alone and then told Holly to stop acting so spoilt.
Holly's eyes grew wide and her mouth hung open. She looked extremely angry.
"What do you mean?! Ivy's the one who's spoilt, not me!"
She started to imitate Ivy's posh London accent.
"Of *course*, I miss the *horses*, but *Daddy* says we might be able to get some new ones *eventually*," she said in an exaggerated accent.
"Why are you being like this?" Daniel asked.
The girlfriend he loved seemed to have changed over the last week, ever since Ivy had come into their lives. He barely recognized this new, angrier and meaner Holly.
"She hasn't done anything to you," he continued.
But the more Daniel stood up for Ivy, the more unreasonable Holly became.

| | |
|---|---|
| spoilt | verzogen, verwöhnt |
| to imitate | nachahmen |
| ϟ posh | vornehm, piekfein |
| exaggerated | übertrieben |
| to stand up for sb. | sich für jmd. einsetzen |
| unreasonable | unvernünftig |

In her English class on Friday afternoon, Holly's head was filled with angry thoughts instead of daydreams. The only thing that she could really find to dislike about Ivy was how pretty she was, and this only made her feel worse.

Holly and her three best friends had been put into a group to discuss a scene in the play *Romeo and Juliet*, but there was only one topic which Holly wanted to discuss.

"She just won't go away!" she hissed.

"Are you *still* talking about Ivy?" asked Emily.

"Poison Ivy, that's what she should be called!" said Holly. She almost seemed to be talking to herself.

"Yeah, so *anyway*... Act three, Scene five..." Emily continued. She hated it when Holly made her look bad in front of her teachers, which, unfortunately, happened rather a lot.

"Why does it upset you so much to spend time with her?" Nina asked.

Emily sighed loudly so that everybody could hear and started writing down some ideas on her own. Holly looked down at the floor.

"I don't know. I just... don't like her."

| | |
|---|---|
| play | *hier:* Theaterstück |
| to hiss | fauchen, zischen |
| Poison Ivy | *hier:* die giftige Ivy (wörtlich: Giftefeu) |
| to stutter | stottern |
| jealous | eifersüchtig |
| to join in | mitmachen |

"I'm sure she only wants to be your friend," said Evie. "She's so far away from her old home and must be missing her own friends. I really don't think she's trying to steal your boyfriend, you know."

"I don't – uh... that's not why I... uh, what's that got to do with anything?" Holly stuttered.

"Oh, come on, Holly. We can all see that you're jealous of her." Even Emily was joining in now.

Holly felt embarrassed, but she could see that there was no point in lying. It was true, she *was* jealous of Ivy. Ivy was so beautiful, and even worse, Daniel seemed to like her.

| | |
|---|---|
| embarrassed | verlegen, peinlich |
| there's no point in | es hat keinen Sinn (zu) |
| might as well | könnte ebenso gut |
| to clear one's throat | sich räuspern |
| to glare | starren |
| cubicle | Kabine |

"The best thing you can do is try to be nice to her," said Evie. "Being jealous isn't going to help anyone, least of all you. Anyway, you have nothing to be jealous about. Dan loves you – he'd never do anything to hurt you."

Holly knew that her friends were right. She decided that if she was going to have to spend so much time with Ivy, she might as well try to be friends with her. From now on she would do her best to be nice to Ivy.

At the front of the room, Mr Stubbs cleared his throat. "So, everyone, you've had fifteen minutes to discuss Act three, Scene five. I want each group to tell me what they think is going on in Juliet's mind during this scene. Let's start with... uh, let's see... Emily's group, over there. What ideas do you have to share with the class?"

Holly's hand shot up immediately. Mr Stubbs gave a look of extreme surprise.

"Yes, Holly?" he said.

"Mr Stubbs, can I go to the bathroom, please?"

The teacher's surprised expression disappeared. "Go on, then."

Emily glared at Holly as she hurried out of the room.

***ÜBUNG 9:** Fill in the blanks. Vervollständige die Sätze mit den angegebenen Wörtern!*

away never missing cleared about discuss

1. There was only one topic that Holly wanted to talk .................................. .
2. Holly wanted Ivy to go .................. .
3. Evie guessed that Ivy was just .................. her friends.
4. Mr Stubbs .................. his throat to get the class's attention.
5. Evie was sure that Dan would .................. do anything to hurt Holly.
6. The girls had to .................. a scene from *Romeo and Juliet.*

Holly sat in the toilet cubicle, wondering whether Mr Stubbs had moved on to another group yet. She was just about to open the door and return to class when she heard a familiar giggle outside the cubicle. Ivy and another girl had just entered the bathroom. Holly thought about saying hello to her and began to open the door.

| | |
|---|---|
| to freeze | *hier:* erstarren |
| how dare | wie kann es ... wagen |
| understanding | verständnisvoll |

"Everything's been going really well between me and Danny so far."

Holly froze. How dare Ivy talk about my boyfriend like that, she thought. And using that horrible, childish nickname as well! Very quietly, she shut the door again and listened. She wanted to find out what else Ivy would say about Daniel.

"He's really understanding. I mean, it's been difficult moving to a completely new part of the country and starting at a new school. I've been quite homesick, but talking to him makes me feel a lot better."

"You're lucky to have someone like that," said the other voice, which Holly did not recognize.
"I am," said Ivy sweetly. "He's perfect, and..." her voice fell to a whisper, "he's the best kisser I've ever met!"
The bathroom filled with the sound of more giggling.

### *ÜBUNG 10: Crossword. Löse das Kreuzworträtsel!*

1. If you say something in a low voice, you say it in a ...
2. If you repeat the first sound of some words when speaking, you ...
3. A short form of your name used by friends.
4. Holly is hiding in a ... in the bathroom.
5. The girls are talking about Ivy during their ... lesson.
6. Daniel thinks that Holly is acting ... towards Ivy.
7. To laugh in a childish way.

Inside the cubicle, Holly's heart felt like it was breaking in two. She could not bear to hear another word, or Ivy's sickening laughter. She held her hands tightly over her ears and waited for the girls to leave. Tears had started to pour silently down her cheeks.

| | |
|---|---|
| to bear sth. | etw. ertragen |
| sickening | ekelhaft, unerträglich |
| to pour down | herabfließen |
| to betray sb. | jmd. betrügen |
| dizzy | schwindelig |
| sob | Schluchzer |
| to comfort sb. | jmd. trösten |

How could Daniel do this to her? She had felt jealous of Ivy, but she had never truly believed that Daniel would betray her like that. Holly felt dizzy with shock and pain.

Long after Ivy had gone, Holly had still not moved and her sobs were getting louder and louder.

Suddenly, she heard a knock.

"Holly! What's wrong? Why haven't you come back to class?"

It was Evie, who sounded very worried.

Holly tried to explain what had happened, but her voice came out broken and weak.

"I can't understand you, Hol. Let me in!" Evie said.

Holly opened the door and Evie hurried to comfort her. Holly told Evie everything that she had heard while Evie listened with an expression of surprise and disappointment.

"But he wouldn't do something like that," Evie said, shaking her head. "I know Dan – he's not that kind of boy."

"That's what I thought, too," Holly managed to say in between sobs.
"Maybe Ivy was lying about it," Evie said. "Perhaps she was trying to make herself look good in front of this other girl... I mean, she hasn't made many new friends here, so she probably just said it to seem cool."

| | |
|---|---|
| target | Ziel |
| to jump to conclusions | voreilige Schlüsse ziehen |
| to sniff | schniefen |
| out of the question | ausgeschlossen |
| to swirl | wirbeln |
| classmate | Klassenkamerad |

Holly finally stopped crying and looked up at Evie. She wanted to believe that what Evie said was the truth.
"But why would she lie about Dan when everyone knows that he's *my* boyfriend?"
"Well... he's the only boy that she's been seen around school with. That makes him the easiest target. Look, Holly, you really need to ask him about this before you jump to conclusions."
"You're right," Holly sniffed. "I'll ask him about it after school. And this time Poison Ivy is *not* walking home with us!"

The rest of the school day went very slowly, and Holly had to fight hard not to cry. Focusing on her lessons was out of the question. Worries swirled around her head, and the thought of what she would say to Daniel after school never left her mind.
Finally, it was time to go home. Evie waited with her until they saw the first of Daniel's classmates leave their last

lesson. Evie wanted to stay with her, but Holly knew that she had to talk to Daniel alone. After some more advice and a hug from Evie, she walked to the school gates, which was where she usually met Daniel.

***ÜBUNG 11:*** *Make the sentence positive. Schreibe die Sätze in nicht verneinte Sätze um!*

1. Evie did not go to the bathroom to find Holly.

..................................................

2. Holly did not try to explain what had happened.

..................................................

3. Evie did not comfort Holly.

..................................................

4. Holly did not want to believe that what Evie said was the truth.

..................................................

..................................................

5. She had never believed that Daniel would not betray her.

..................................................

6. Evie didn't say, "Don't let me in!"

..................................................

Holly waited nervously for five minutes. Daniel was not usually late leaving school, but by now all of his classmates seemed to have left. Five minutes soon became ten. She checked her mobile phone, which she kept on silent while she was at school so that she would not get into trouble. The small screen flashed with a new message.

> Hey beautiful. So sorry I can't meet u this afternoon – going 2 town 2 show Ivy around. I'll make it up 2 u later, I promise! Love u xxx

Holly's body froze with shock and confusion, and for a moment she could not breathe. Her chest felt tight and hot, and her mind filled with questions. Could Daniel, her sweet, kind boyfriend Daniel, really be two-timing her with Ivy? His romantic words and promises made the thought seem so much worse – if he was really betraying her, then why was he pretending that he still loved her? Why was he so cruel?

She had to find out the truth. Quickly, Holly punched a number into the keypad.

"Oh, hey Holly!"

| | |
|---|---|
| hug | Umarmung |
| on silent | auf lautlos |
| to flash | aufleuchten, blinken |
| chest | Brust |
| ϟ to two-time sb. | jmd. betrügen |
| to pretend | vormachen, vorgeben |
| to punch | *hier:* eintippen |
| keypad | Tastenfeld |

*ÜBUNG 12: Match-up. Verbinde die Gegensatzpaare!*

| | |
|---|---|
| 1. froze | loose |
| 2. nervously | better |
| 3. silent | confidently |
| 4. beautiful | melted |
| 5. tight | loud |
| 6. worse | ugly |

The smile that Holly could hear in Daniel's voice now made her feel sick. How long had he been pretending like this?
"Did you get my text?" he asked.
"Yes, I did," said Holly coldly. "But what I would really like to know is what *exactly* you are doing in town with Ivy."
The silence on the other end of the phone lasted slightly too long. "Um, I... uh, I'm just showing her... um, some... stuff," he finished lamely.

| | |
|---|---|
| text (message) | SMS |
| lamely | lahm, schwach |
| relieved | erleichtert |
| to become a blur | verschwimmen |

Holly could hear the snake-like whisper of a girl's voice in the background. It sounded like she was trying to tell him what to say.
"What kind of stuff?" she asked Daniel.

More silence. "Just... all the things to do in the town centre." Daniel sounded relieved to have found the words. "...because... she didn't think there was much to do around here, you remember?"
Holly felt too angry to be upset anymore. She had heard enough: Daniel's excuses could not hide the ugly truth.
"You're a terrible liar, you know," she said and hung up the phone without waiting to hear a reply.
As she walked to her house, the anger that had held back the tears started to break under the weight of her sadness and pain. She usually walked home with Daniel, and now, as she walked alone, it was impossible not to think of him. She saw the field where they had kicked fallen leaves in the autumn and the bench where they had sat hand in hand. Had it really meant so little to him that he could betray her with his cruel kisses and lies?

Holly turned the corner and started walking down her street. By now, the familiar sights of the walk home had become a blur behind the tears that filled her eyes. At least she could not see Daniel's house at the end of the road through the blur.

She opened the front door and ran upstairs to her bedroom. Tears fell down her cheeks and onto the bed as her body shook with sobs.

A hundred thoughts and angry questions swirled around her head and would not go away. But one thought cut through the confusion: she had no choice but to break up with Daniel. She picked up her phone and began to write a message. Her hands trembled as she typed the words.

| | |
|---|---|
| to tremble | zittern |
| to deserve sth. | etw. verdient haben |
| to wail | heulen, jammern |
| to curl into a ball | sich zusammenrollen, sich einigeln |

It's over between us. Don't try 2 call me or speak 2 me because nothing can change my mind.

After what he had done, Daniel did not deserve an explanation or a second chance. He would only hurt her again. She wanted her message to sound like she did not care, even though the truth was that she could barely read it through her tears. She stared at the message for a long time. As she sent it, Holly wailed even louder and curled into a ball on the bed. She lay there for hours, still crying, until she finally fell asleep.

3

# The Cold Shoulder

# 3

Holly hat mit Daniel Schluss gemacht und will nie wieder mit ihm reden! Aber alles in ihrem Zimmer erinnert sie daran, wie glücklich sie mit Daniel war. Ihre Freundinnen versuchen sie zu trösten und versprechen ihr, Daniel die kalte Schulter zu zeigen. Mit einer Shoppingtour wollen sie Holly ablenken, aber Holly fühlt sich dick und unattraktiv. Kein Wunder, dass Daniel sie für die schlanke Ivy verlassen hat!
Dass Holly ihm in der Schule nicht aus dem Weg gehen kann, macht alles nur noch schlimmer. Und dann sieht sie ihn ausgerechnet neben Ivy am Schultor …

The sound of a ringing phone shattered Holly's dream. Her thoughts were still fuzzy from sleep, so that for a moment she did not remember where she was or what had happened. She was soon reminded when she saw the caller's name appear on the screen of her mobile phone: Dan. The memory hit her like a punch in the stomach.
She rejected the call immediately and stood up from her bed. In the mirror in front of her, she saw somebody she barely recognized: a girl in a crumpled school uniform with black smudges of make-up on her cheeks.

Her mobile phone rang again. Holly's face twisted in anger, and she threw the phone onto the bed as hard as she could. Why can't he just leave me alone, she thought. It was the only thing she had asked him to do.

| | |
|---|---|
| fuzzy | unklar, verschwommen |
| to reject sth. | etw. ablehnen |
| crumpled | zerknittert |
| smudge | Schmierfleck |
| to twist | (das Gesicht) verziehen |
| reminder | Andenken, Erinnerung |
| to torment | quälen |
| to tear | (zer)reißen |
| carelessly | achtlos |

All around the room there were more cruel reminders of Daniel to torment her. Photographs, gifts and love letters stared at her from every wall. She had carefully put them up, had enjoyed looking at them while daydreaming about Daniel. Now she tore them down quickly and carelessly.

| | |
|---|---|
| to fall apart | in die Brüche gehen |
| ruined | zerstört, ruiniert |
| to burst into tears | in Tränen ausbrechen |
| Tears welled up in her eyes. | Ihr stiegen Tränen in die Augen. |

When she had finished, Holly put all the things that she had torn down into a box, which she hid under her bed. She could not bring herself to throw them away. Not yet.

Holly had never expected her relationship to fall apart so painfully. She had been so happy with Daniel, but now her favourite memories were all ruined. She felt stupid for believing that he had ever truly loved her. That feeling grew worse when she remembered all the times that she had told her friends about her perfect relationship: now she would have to tell them something very different.

Holly picked up the phone. She did not want to call her friends, but she knew that she would have to tell them eventually. At least they might be able to help her to feel a bit better if she invited them to her house the next day.

She began to dial Evie's number, but burst into tears before she had typed half of it. Instead, she typed a message and sent it to each of her three best friends. Somehow it was easier to write down what had happened than to say the terrible words out loud.

Holly lay back down on her bed and stared at the ceiling. Tears welled up in her eyes and made everything look fuzzy. She felt like nothing in the world could make her feel better, but she knew that seeing her three best friends would at least be a good start.

*ÜBUNG 13: Multiple choice. Kreuze jeweils die richtige Variante an!*

1. Holly's mobile phone...
   a) ❑ ringed.
   b) ❑ rhung.
   c) ❑ rang.

2. Holly...
   a) ❑ tore down
   b) ❑ tore up
   c) ❑ tore through

   the photographs on her wall.

3. Holly did not want to tell her friends that she and Dan had...
   a) ❑ cheated.
   b) ❑ broken up.
   c) ❑ gone out.

4. Tears...
   a) ❑ burst
   b) ❑ rolled
   c) ❑ welled

   down Holly's cheeks.

5. Holly hadn't expected her relationship to...
   a) ❑ fall away
   b) ❑ fall up
   c) ❑ fall apart

   so painfully.

| | |
|---|---|
| to gather | sich versammeln |
| to blow one's nose | sich die Nase putzen |
| tissue | (Papier-)Taschentuch |
| to imagine sth. | sich etw. vorstellen (können) |
| to cheat (on sb.) | jmd. betrügen |
| to silence | zum Schweigen bringen |

The next day, Holly's friends were gathered around her in the living room of her house.

"I just can't believe it," said Emily.

She shook her head from side to side and looked at Holly as though she was about to tell her it was just a bad joke.

"I know," Holly sniffed, before blowing her nose on a tissue that was already wet from her tears. "I never imagined that this could happen."

Evie was silent for a moment. She looked down at the ground and said, "I'm so sorry, Hol. I feel awful that I gave you the wrong advice yesterday – it's just that Dan was the last person I would have expected to cheat. I thought he was such a nice guy."

"And you seemed like the perfect couple," said Nina. "I'm so shocked – how can this be true?"

The room became quiet. Holly's phone began ringing loudly, but she silenced it quickly instead of answering.

"Who was that?" asked Evie.

"Dan," Holly answered. "He keeps calling me. It's like he wants to torment me. Isn't it enough for him that he's already broken my heart?"

She began to cry again.

The other girls gathered closer around to comfort her.

| | |
|---|---|
| Poor him! | Der Arme! |
| ↯ to give sb. the cold shoulder | jmd. die kalte Schulter zeigen |
| uneasy | angespannt, unbehaglich |
| to support sb. | jmd. unterstützen |

"He called me yesterday, too," said Evie.

Holly looked up from her tissue and listened.

"Of course, I didn't know you had broken up with him, so I answered. He sounded kind of upset and was asking if I knew where you were because he wanted to speak to you. I thought it was pretty strange at the time, but then I got your text and that explained everything. He really did sound upset, though."

"*He's* upset?!" shouted Holly. "Well, that really is too bad. Poor him!" she added sarcastically.

Her voice shook with emotion.

"Have you spoken to him since you broke up?" Emily asked after a pause.

"No, and I'm not going to," Holly replied. "I'm not going to let him see how much he's upset me. And if you're my true friends, you won't either."

"What do you mean?" asked Nina.

"I mean, if he tries to speak to you at school, ignore him. Just give him the cold shoulder. And if he calls you or asks you to give me a message, please don't even mention it to me – I just want to forget all about him."

The others looked a little uneasy, but they had no choice. They agreed to her plan. If ignoring Daniel was Holly's way of getting over her hurt, then they would support her.

*ÜBUNG 14: Unscramble the sentences! Bilde ganze Sätze aus den durcheinander geratenen Satzteilen!*

1. too – me – yesterday – he called

..................................................................

2. and – the ceiling – lay down – Holly – stared at – on her bed

..................................................................

..................................................................

3. upset me – going to – let him – I am not – how much – see – he has

..................................................................

..................................................................

4. Holly – to give Dan – them – told – the cold shoulder

..................................................................

..................................................................

5. that I – the wrong advice – I feel – gave you – awful – yesterday

..................................................................

..................................................................

| | |
|---|---|
| to take sb.'s mind off sth. | jmd. von etw. ablenken |
| window display | Schaufenster-auslage |
| to glow | strahlen, scheinen |
| tinsel | Lametta, Flitter |
| cheerful | fröhlich |
| elf | Elfe |
| merry | fröhlich, vergnügt |
| sympathetically | verständnisvoll |
| flicker | Anflug, Schimmer |

The next day was a Sunday and the girls decided to go shopping in the town centre to take Holly's mind off Daniel. They walked along the high street, where the front of every shop reminded them that Christmas was coming. Window displays glowed with bright lights, and tinsel covered the tables and bookshelves inside. Christmas music was playing everywhere. The cheerful melodies left Holly's heart feeling even colder.

"I hate Christmas," she said.

"No, you don't!" Emily told her. "Last Christmas you said it was your favourite time of the year. You even had a big Christmas party and dressed up as an elf! Don't you remember?"

"Well, I hate *this* Christmas anyway," Holly said. "I don't feel very merry."

"Of course you don't," said Evie sympathetically. "But maybe we can help! Let's see if we can get some ideas for Christmas presents... how about over there?" She pointed at Holly's favourite clothes shop.

A flicker of a smile showed on Holly's face and then disappeared again. The window display was full of clothes in her favourite colour, pink.

As they walked closer to the shop, Holly's eyes focused on a bright pink dress. It was perfect. She could imagine herself wearing it at a party...

"Who's that girl?" all the boys would ask.

And Daniel, alone in the corner, would watch jealously as the beautiful girl in the pink dress laughed and flirted without noticing him at all.

Holly snapped out of her daydream. She searched for the dress inside the shop and was pleased when she finally found it in her size. Nina and Emily also chose some clothes to try on, but Evie looked a little bored. She had suggested the shop to make Holly happy, but she was not really very interested in clothes unless they were sports kits. Eventually, she found a nice shirt to try on so that she could go with the others to the changing room.

| | |
|---|---|
| to snap | *hier:* hochschrecken |
| to suggest | vorschlagen |
| ϟ kit | Klamotten |
| changing room | Umkleidekabine |

*ÜBUNG 15: Friends forever? Finde heraus, ob du Freunde fürs Leben hast!*

1. What is the main thing that you and your friends have in common?
   a) ❑ We're all pretty and popular.
   b) ❑ We have similar interests and hobbies.
   c) ❑ We like the same music.

2. If you had a painful break-up like Holly's, how would your friends act?
   a) ❑ They would probably ask my ex-boyfriend out on a date.
   b) ❑ They would support me and try to make me feel better.
   c) ❑ They would not mention it at all to help me to forget about my problems.

3. What are your friends' future plans like?
   a) ❑ I don't know – I've never asked.
   b) ❑ Quite similar to mine.
   c) ❑ Very different to my dreams for the future, but I support them.

4. Would you be upset if you had an argument with one of your friends?
   a) ❑ Of course not – we have arguments all the time.
   b) ❑ Very. I would try my best to put things right as soon as possible.
   c) ❑ Yes. And if it was my fault, I would apologize.

| | |
|---|---|
| zip | Reißverschluss |
| bulge | Wölbung |
| stubbornly | hartnäckig |
| lopsidedly | schief, ungleich |
| let alone | geschweige denn |
| to bump into sb. | mit jmd. zusammenstoßen |
| to twirl | sich drehen, wirbeln |
| flatly | *hier:* ausdruckslos |
| to go on a diet | eine Diät machen |

Inside the changing room, Holly undressed and excitedly began to put on the beautiful pink dress. But when she tried to pull up the zip, it stopped half way and would not move any further. She tried again, but still the zip reached the same point, where a bulge of her skin stubbornly stood in its way. She looked into the mirror and sighed deeply at her reflection. The dress was much too tight around her stomach and hung down lopsidedly below her knees. It looked completely different to how it had appeared in the window, let alone in her daydream. All of a sudden, she felt very unattractive. No wonder Dan wanted to be with Ivy instead of me, she thought.

She pulled on her clothes and began to leave the changing room, but when she stepped out, she bumped into Nina. Nina was wearing a light yellow dress which made her look even more beautiful than usual. She was twirling around by the mirror and asking Evie what she thought of the outfit.

"Oh, Holly, it's you!" she said as she saw her friend's reflection in the mirror in front of her. She turned around and asked, "Are you going to buy that lovely dress?"

"No," Holly replied flatly. "I'm going on a diet instead."

"Don't be silly, Holly!" said Evie. "You don't need to go on a diet at all."

Emily suddenly stepped out from behind a curtain where she had been changing. It seemed she had an opinion on the subject, too. She was wearing a purple top which suited her dark hair beautifully – and which made Holly feel even worse.

"You're the perfect size, Holly!" Emily said.

"That's easy for all of you to say. You're all tiny! I'm so much fatter than you."

"No, you really aren't!" Evie argued.

She was not lying. Holly was only slightly larger than the other girls, and was certainly not fat.

"Well, it doesn't matter anyway because you can't change my mind. I've decided that I'm going on a diet!" Holly said and walked away from the changing rooms.

The sound of ringing followed her again, but this time she did not even take the phone out of her bag.

The walk home was slightly awkward. Emily and Nina both carried shopping bags containing the clothes they had bought, while Holly walked beside them unhappily. She was almost silent until they passed another shop.

"Do you think they sell Jupiter Bars in there?" Holly asked.

The other girls did not mention her diet as Holly went inside to buy a large bar of chocolate.

*ÜBUNG 16: Articles. Setze den richtigen Artikel a, an oder the ein!*

1. Nina tried on ............... outfit that made her look even more beautiful than usual.

2. Emily wore ............... purple top that really suited her.

3. Meanwhile, ............... dress that Holly tried on was too small for her.

4. This made her decide to go on ............... diet.

5. They all left ............... changing room.

6. ............... walk home was a bit awkward.

7. Their shopping trip lasted ............... hour.

The next week, things did not get any better. Holly still felt so unhappy that she found it difficult to get up in the mornings. Every day she dreaded bumping into Daniel on the walk to school or seeing him at the school gates. She even switched off her mobile phone all week because she could not bear for him to call one more time.

The other girls tried to make her feel better but by the end of the week they were beginning to worry. They knew that Holly was very romantic and took relationships seriously, but they had never seen her so upset over a boy before. She seemed to have lost all of her confidence.

They were so angry about what Daniel had done to Holly that it was quite easy to do as she had asked and give him the cold shoulder.

Evie found it the most difficult because she had to play football with him every week. However, if Daniel tried to speak to her, Evie simply thought about how much her friend had changed since he had cheated on her. This always made her very angry. The only problem with this technique was that it got her into trouble with the football coach – Evie sometimes found herself tackling Daniel on the football field even though they were in the same team.

| | |
|---|---|
| to dread sth. | große Angst haben vor |
| confidence | Selbstbewusstsein |
| to tackle | angreifen (Fußball) |

The next week was a little better. Holly tried very hard not to think about Daniel or how happy she had been with him. Instead she tried to focus on school and her friends. Without all of her daydreams to distract her, Holly began to understand more of her lessons and to get better marks for her homework. She had always enjoyed English lessons, and now she was really paying attention to *Romeo and Juliet* – another love story ending in tragedy. She soon found herself becoming more and more lost in the beautiful, poetic language of the play.

| | |
|---|---|
| to distract sb. | jmd. ablenken |
| diary entry | Tagebucheintrag |
| vivid imagination | lebhafte Fantasie |
| break-up | Trennung |

So when the class was asked to write a diary entry through the eyes of Juliet, Holly was sure she could do a good job. With her vivid imagination, she found it easy to bring the characters' thoughts and feelings to life; it was as if they were real people she knew. In the end, her diary entry was so good that Mr Stubbs gave her the highest mark possible and read out her work in front of the whole class.

That afternoon she was beginning to feel the first flickers of happiness since her break-up with Daniel. They would not last long.

*ÜBUNG 17: Short forms. Setze die richtige Kurzform ein!*

1. Holly *(could not)* ...................... get up easily in the mornings.

2. Holly's friends *(had not)* .................... seen her so upset over a boy before.

3. The first flickers of Holly's happiness *(would not)* ........................ last long.

4. "I *(cannot)* ........................... believe what happened."

5. "You *(should not)* ...................... have tackled Daniel – *(he is)* .................. in your team!"

6. "*(You have)* ..................... said enough!"

Holly and her friends were about to walk home later that afternoon. As they passed the school gate, Holly saw Daniel, with Ivy by his side. For a moment, Holly found it difficult to breathe. She could feel her heart pounding in her chest and her mouth becoming dry.

The other girls noticed the scene soon after.

"Ignore them," Evie said defiantly and put her arm around Holly to walk away from school with her.

"I can't believe it," said Emily. "I mean, flaunting his new relationship like that, right in front of you – it's disgusting."

"It's like he wants to hurt you even more, when you've done nothing wrong. What a creep," added Nina.

Holly tried to fight the tears that were beginning to well up in her eyes. She looked away from the couple, but her friends did not. Instead they glared angrily at Daniel and Ivy for a long time as they walked past the gates.

Daniel watched the girls pass by with their cold, hard expressions. He wanted to go up and speak to Holly, but the anger that he saw in the faces of her friends told him that it would not be a good idea. He sat down on the low wall by the gate and put his head in his hands.

| | |
|---|---|
| to pound | pochen, schlagen |
| defiantly | kämpferisch, trotzig |
| to flaunt sth. | etw. zur Schau stellen, protzen |
| disgusting | widerlich |
| ϟ creep | Widerling |
| sensitive | verständnisvoll, sensibel |

"What have I done to make her hate me so much?" he said.
"I can't imagine," said Ivy sympathetically. "I mean, it was her who broke up with *you*, right?"
She was about to continue, but the sound of her mobile phone ringing interrupted her.
"Sorry, I'll just answer this," she said and took the phone out of her coat pocket.
Although she wanted to be sensitive to Daniel, she could not hide the huge smile that spread across her face when she saw the name of the caller. She put the phone to her ear.
"Danny!" she answered. "How are you, baby? I've been missing you so much."

Daniel did not listen to Ivy or the muffled voice on the other end of the phone. His mind was elsewhere, and the last thing he wanted to hear was Ivy talking yet again about her how much she missed her boyfriend in London.

| | |
|---|---|
| muffled | gedämpft, leise |

Hopelessly, he watched Holly and her friends disappear into the distance.

*ÜBUNG 18: Put the events in order. Bringe die Sätze in die richtige Reihenfolge!*

a) Ivy answers the phone.
b) Holly sees Dan and Ivy.
c) Dan tries to ignore Ivy's telephone conversation with her boyfriend.
d) Dan puts his head in his hands.
e) Holly's friends tell her to ignore Dan.
f) Holly feels her heart pounding and her mouth becoming dry.
g) Dan wants to speak to Holly but stays silent because he sees how angry her friends are.

| 1 | 2 | 3 | 4 | 5 | 6 | 7 |
|---|---|---|---|---|---|---|
| b | | | | | | |

4

# Food for Thought

# 4

Es ist Anfang Dezember und Holly ist so gar nicht in Adventsstimmung. Einfach jede Kleinigkeit erinnert sie an Daniel, sie kann einfach nicht aufhören an ihn zu denken.
Doch mit einer neuen Frisur gewinnt Holly ganz langsam ihr Selbstvertrauen zurück und beschließt, sich voll in die Vorbereitungen zum Weihnachtsmarkt der Schule zu stürzen, um endlich auf andere Gedanken zu kommen. Zusammen mit ihren Freundinnen will sie einen Stand mit deutschen Spezialitäten präsentieren – so vergeht die Vorweihnachtszeit mit Plätzchenbacken und Punschtrinken …

Holly picked up her Advent calendar and carefully pulled back a tiny door marked with the number one. It was the first day of December and her mother had given her the calendar that morning, just like she did every year. Inside, there was a small piece of chocolate and a picture of a tree in a beautiful, snow-covered landscape. When she saw it, Holly was painfully reminded of the

| | |
|---|---|
| food for thought | Stoff zum Nachdenken |
| sb.'s heart sinks | jmd. wird das Herz schwer |
| festive | festlich, weihnachtlich |

fun and laughter that she and Daniel had shared on that snowy day less than a month before. It felt like so much time had passed since then.

Her heart sank as she closed the door and looked away. "Thanks for the Advent calendar, Mum," she said quietly.

Her mother was clearly in a festive mood. She was walking around the house so lightly that she almost seemed to be dancing. Both of Holly's parents loved Christmas, as did Holly usually. But this year she could not get excited about the beginning of Advent.

Even the merry sound of the Christmas songs playing on the radio made her cringe a little inside.

Her mum came over and put a hand on her shoulder.

"How about a nice mince pie to cheer you up? I made them for us to eat after dinner, but you can have one now."

"No thanks, I'm on a diet," Holly replied and pushed away the plate of warm pies that her mother had placed in front of her.

Holly's mum looked worried. She knew that Holly and Daniel had broken up, and had tried ever since to do and say the right things to make her daughter feel better. But nothing had worked.

"You don't need to go on a diet, love," Holly's mum said soothingly. "You're perfect as you are."

| | |
|---|---|
| mince pie | Kuchen mit einer Füllung aus Dörrobst und Sirup |
| soothingly | besänftigend |
| to surround | umgeben |
| hint | Spur, Andeutung |
| to echo sth. | etw. wiederholen |
| to admire | bewundern |

Her daughter's body felt awkward at first when she moved to hug her, but after a moment Holly relaxed and let her mum's arms surround her. It felt so warm and comforting that she did not want to let go.

"I know something that will cheer you up more than a mince pie," her mum said eventually. "Come with me. I'm taking you for an early Christmas present."

*ÜBUNG 19: Find the mistake. Finde den Fehler in jedem Satz und schreibe den Satz korrekt auf!*

1. Holly's mum came and put her hand in her daughter's shoulder.

..................................................................

2. She offered Holly an mince pie.

..................................................................

3. Holly refused because she was having a diet.

..................................................................

4. Holly's mum told her she did not need of be on a diet.

..................................................................

5. Holly's mum decided to cheer Holly up with an early christmas present.

..................................................................

The next day, Holly arrived at school and walked into the classroom with just a hint of a smile.

"Wow, look at your hair!" said Nina, who was the first to see her. Evie and Emily both echoed her a second later.

"It really suits you," said Evie as she admired Holly's new shoulder-length bob.

"Thanks," Holly replied. "My mum took me to the new hairdresser's in town. It was amazing – they treated me like a film star!"
"You *look* like a film star!" Emily said.
Holly flicked her hair and gave her friends a Hollywood smile. The others laughed and continued telling her how wonderful she looked.
However, it was not long before they had to return to their usual school routine and be quiet while their form tutor, Mrs Skelton, called out their names. Once everybody had answered, Mrs Skelton started to tell the class about the Christmas market that was going to take place at the school just before the Christmas holidays. Holly was in a good mood that day, so she did not try to ignore this reminder of the festive season. Instead, it gave her an idea.
The teacher told the class that they could talk quietly for five minutes before their first lesson began. The girls immediately started talking about Holly's new haircut again, but Holly changed the subject.
"Nina, you know Germany..." she began.
"Err... yeah," Nina replied sarcastically. "I've heard of it." Nina was German.
"Well, I was just thinking about the Christmas market. It would be really cool if there was a German stall there. Everyone could get a chance to see what Christmas is like in Germany."
"That's a great idea," said Nina. "Christmas markets are a German tradition, after all."
"Really?" Holly asked. "I didn't know that."

She realized as she spoke that she knew almost nothing about traditions outside of England, although one of her best friends was from another country.

"Maybe *we* could have a stall," Holly continued. "I know that parents and teachers normally run the market stalls, but do you think they'd let us?"

"Perhaps. There's only one way to find out," Nina replied.

She walked straight up to the front of the class to ask the teacher, while the others waited hopefully for the answer.

| | |
|---|---|
| hairdresser's | Friseur(laden) |
| to flick one's hair | die Haare nach hinten werfen |
| routine | *hier:* Alltag |
| form tutor | Klassenlehrerin |
| stall | Stand |
| to be drowned out | übertönt werden |
| blank | ausdruckslos |

They all agreed that this would be the perfect opportunity for Nina to share a part of her culture with the rest of the school. They tried to hear what Mrs Skelton was saying, but her words were drowned out by the voices of their classmates.

When Nina returned, her smile told them the answer before she said a word.

"Well, we've got our stall! We just need to decide on our prices and how much to make, and then we have to show Mrs Skelton some examples of all the things we're going to sell."

"So... uh, what are we going to sell?" asked Evie.

She turned to Holly, whose idea the stall had been, but her expression was blank. Holly did not usually think about the details before saying her ideas out loud.

Luckily, Nina already had something in mind.

"I told Mrs Skelton we'd sell some traditional food and drink – like a real German Christmas market. Don't worry, I can think of lots of things. And she said that we can even keep all the money that we make!"

"Brilliant!" said Emily. "But I'm surprised that Mrs Skelton agreed to it so easily."

Nina could explain. "She said that she knew she could trust me because of German Club."

Nina had started the club earlier that year to teach German to some other pupils. She had shown herself to be a very reliable teacher: she was always on time and carefully planned her lessons to make learning the language fun and interesting. It was no surprise that she had earned Mrs Skelton's trust.

During the next two days, all that the girls could talk about was their stall at the Christmas market. The long conversations about German Christmas traditions gave Holly a chance to find out a lot more about Nina and the country that she came from.

"So what do you think we should sell then?" Nina asked the others on their way home from school.

"Um... I can't remember how to say it..." Holly began.

| | |
|---|---|
| to trust | vertrauen |
| reliable | zuverlässig |
| to earn sb.'s trust | jmd.s Vertrauen gewinnen |
| swirl | Gewirr |

*ÜBUNG 20: True or false? Kreuze die richtigen Aussagen an!*

1. Holly knew exactly what they should sell on their stall. ☐
2. Nina tricked Mrs Skelton into agreeing to let the girls have a stall at the Christmas market. ☐
3. The girls had to give all the money they made at the market to the school. ☐
4. Holly's friends all liked her new haircut. ☐
5. Most of the stalls at the market were run by pupils. ☐
6. Nina was a very reliable teacher. ☐
7. Nina did not want to ask Mrs Skelton about the Christmas market. ☐

Nina had only just finished telling them about some traditional types of food and drink, but by now all Holly could remember was a swirl of strange German words.
"Those, uh, biscuit things sounded really good."
"*Lebkuchen?*" suggested Nina.
"Yeah, that's it," Holly replied. "*Lebkuchen.*"
The foreign sounds felt unfamiliar in her mouth.

| | |
|---|---|
| stocking | Strumpf |
| Father Christmas | Weihnachtsmann |
| Christmas Eve | Heiligabend |
| Christmas Day | erster Weihnachtsfeiertag |

"I think that *Punsch* would be popular, too," said Evie.

"Well, whatever we're going to sell, we really need to practise making it this week," Emily said. "I don't want to let the teachers down."

"This week?" Nina responded. "But it's almost... um... I don't know what the word is in English. 'Nicholas'?"

"Nicholas? That's a name, not a day," said Evie, looking confused.

"Oh, you know... the sixth of December?"

The others still did not understand.

"In Germany, it's called *Nikolaus*," Nina explained. "Children put out a boot for Saint Nicholas and in the morning it's filled with little presents and sweets. Don't you have anything like that in England?"

"We leave stockings out for Father Christmas on Christmas Eve and open them on Christmas Day," Holly replied. "But that's ages away. Is Christmas Day the sixth of December in Germany then?"

She realized there was still a lot she did not know about Nina's Christmas traditions.

"No, we also open presents on the twenty-fourth of December," Nina said. "*Nikolaus* is just for kids. My sister's really excited about it – she's been polishing her boot all week!"

"What?" asked Evie. "This is getting more and more confusing!"

"You have to polish the boot before you leave it out to show that you've been good."

"Ah," said Emily, beginning to understand. "So that Saint Nicholas doesn't give you coal instead of presents."

"Coal? No!" said Nina. "If you've been bad, you get a switch."

Holly was surprised by how differently Christmas was celebrated in Germany, but she found it extremely interesting.

"When should we practise cooking then?" she asked. She secretly hoped that Nina would invite them to her house so that they could find out more.

"How about this weekend?" Emily suggested.

| | |
|---|---|
| to polish | polieren, putzen |
| coal | Kohle |
| switch | *hier:* Rute |
| That's fine by me. | Das passt mir gut. |
| ingredients | Zutaten |

"That's fine by me," Nina replied. "Why don't you all come round to my house on Saturday and I'll make sure we have all the ingredients we need.

"Perfect!" said Holly happily. She could not wait.

*ÜBUNG 21: Find the solution. Enträtsele die Definitionen und finde das Lösungswort!*

1. December 24th.
2. In England, you get this in your stocking if you have been bad.
3. Things you mix together when cooking.
4. Evie is not interested in clothes, unless they are sports ...
5. Holly normally loved Christmas, but this year she was not in a ... mood.
6. Nina had earned Mrs Skelton's ...

1. .... H .... .... .... T ▮ .... .... .... V ....

2. C .... ▮ ....

3. .... .... G ▮ .... D .... .... N T ....

4. ▮ .... T ....

5. .... ▮ .... .... .... V ....

6. .... .... .... S ▮

Lösung: .... .... .... .... .... ....

| | |
|---|---|
| at once | *hier:* zugleich |
| Advent wreath | Adventskranz |
| gaudy | knallbunt |
| nutcracker | Nussknacker |
| to be used to sth. | etw. gewohnt sein |

On Saturday, the girls met at Nina's house. When she stepped into the decorated living room, Holly felt that everything around her was at once strange and familiar. The Advent wreathes, red candles and wooden decorations looked similar to things that she recognized, but different at the same time. Her own living room was full of tinsel. It had gaudy strings of bright plastic hanging from the ceiling and flashing neon lights. But Nina's living room looked more traditional, like something from a film. There were nutcrackers and a lot of wooden toys, and candles instead of the neon lights that Holly was used to. There was just one thing missing.

"Where's your Christmas tree?" Holly asked.

"The Christmas tree?" said Nina. "It's far too early for that!"

"You get presents on the sixth of December but it's too *early* to put up a Christmas tree?!" Evie asked in surprise. "I'll never understand Christmas in Germany!"

"We haven't got a Christmas tree at home yet either," Emily said. "My parents don't put ours up until a week before Christmas."

"That's still too early for us," Nina explained. "In our family we usually wait until Christmas Eve."

*ÜBUNG 22: Are you traditional? Magst du Traditionen?*

1. When do you prefer to put up the Christmas tree?
   a) ❑ I would never dream of putting it up before Christmas Eve.
   b) ❑ Whenever. I wouldn't even mind not having one at all.
   c) ❑ Sometime during Advent.

2. How do you celebrate special holidays such as Easter?
   a) ❑ I do the same thing every year to celebrate and I would hate for it to be any different.
   b) ❑ I don't. They're just like any other day.
   c) ❑ I usually spend it with my family.

3. If you imagine your future wedding, what does it look like?
   a) ❑ I am wearing a white dress and am getting married in a church.
   b) ❑ I don't want to get married.
   c) ❑ I'm getting married in Las Vegas.

Just like she had promised, Nina had got all of the ingredients ready to make a few different kinds of food and some *Punsch*. The girls began to follow Nina's instructions and had soon made a variety of types and flavours of dough, which they then shaped into balls, stars and hearts. Nobody was surprised when, at the end, the area where Holly had been working was by far the messiest. She had spilled flour all over the floor, where it had later been joined by some broken eggshells and cinnamon from one of the recipes. She even had a little bit of flour on her nose, which made the others giggle.

"Holly, are you mixing your dough in the bowl or on the floor?" Nina laughed.

"One thing's for sure – we shouldn't let you anywhere near the oven!" Emily added.

Sure enough, Emily and Nina put the biscuits, cakes and pastries into the oven while Holly tried her best to clean up the mess that she had made. Once everything was beginning to bake nicely, the girls started making the *Punsch*. The delicious smells that came from each ingredient soon filled the kitchen with an unmistakably festive aroma.

| | |
|---|---|
| flavour | Sorte, Geschmacksrichtung |
| dough | Teig |
| cinnamon | Zimt |
| recipe | Kochrezept |
| oven | Ofen |
| sure enough | tatsächlich |
| pastry | Gebäck |
| unmistakably | unverkennbar |

"It's delicious!" Holly said as she tried a small amount, and then poured herself a whole glass.

"Let me try a bit," Nina said. She drank the warming *Punsch*, closed her eyes and smiled. "Mmm, it tastes like Christmas."

It was a little while before they noticed the smell of burning that was mingling with the aroma of fruit and cinnamon.

"Oh no, quick!" cried Nina and pulled open the oven door. What was inside was black on top and looked just as burnt as it smelled.

Holly held her hands up in an innocent pose.

"Nothing to do with me this time!" she said.

Luckily, there was still more dough left, so they threw away the tray of blackened biscuits and prepared another one. This time, they were careful not to leave it in the oven for too long.

Once it was ready, Emily opened the oven and took out the tray. Now the smell that wafted from the oven was sweet and spicy.

| | |
|---|---|
| to mingle | sich vermischen |
| innocent pose | Unschuldsgeste |
| tray | *hier:* Backblech |
| spicy | würzig |
| to stuff | stopfen |
| ϟ to go (all) soppy on sb. | rührselig werden |

"What about your diet?" Evie joked to Holly as they all began trying the food they had made.

"You know, I've decided I don't need to go on a diet," Holly replied, and then stuffed a hot *Plaetzchen* into her mouth whole. "I'm fine as I am."

"I'm so glad you finally agree with the rest of us," said Emily.

Holly realized that, for the first time in weeks, she was feeling happy. She had not even thought about Daniel once during the time that she had spent with her friends that day.

"This has been such a nice day," she told the others. "You're the best friends I could ever have..."

"No need to go all soppy on us!" Evie joked.

"I mean it, though," Holly said.

The few biscuits and cakes that had escaped the girls' mouths had now cooled down, so Nina put them into a box. She was going to take them into school to show Mrs Skelton on Monday morning.

The girls chatted happily about the market, school, their favourite pop stars and their plans for the Christmas holidays. There was only one subject that they avoided. Evie, Nina and Emily knew that Holly's feelings were still raw, so they did not mention their boyfriends and crushes, and certainly did not mention Daniel.

It was only when Holly left the house that she allowed her thoughts to return to memories of Daniel. But now she felt able to look at them with clearer eyes. Although she still felt a stab of pain when she remembered the happy times they had spent together, she also imagined other scenes. Holly and Daniel danced together through her mind... but now she also saw her friends, who were disappointed, wondering where she could be. Then she remembered them walking away without her.

| | |
|---|---|
| to avoid | (ver)meiden |
| raw | *hier:* empfindlich, blank |
| ⚡ crush | Schwarm |
| stab of pain | stechender Schmerz |
| to neglect | vernachlässigen |

Holly finally realized how much she had neglected her closest friends during her relationship with Daniel. She promised herself that she would never again forget how important they were.

*ÜBUNG 23: Reading comprehension. Beantworte die Fragen zum Text!*

1. What did Holly spill on the floor?

..............................................................

2. What happened to the first tray of biscuits?

..............................................................

3. How did they avoid this happening again?

..............................................................

4. Why did Nina put the leftover food into a box?

..............................................................

5. How did the smells change in the kitchen?

..............................................................

..............................................................

6. What did Holly promise herself?

..............................................................

After the girls had finished making their food and drink, Emily walked back to her house through the park. While she was staring into the distance, she noticed Daniel playing football with some friends. Emily began to glare at him coldly , but she was not very good at being mean to people. She was pretending that she had not seen him by looking the other way, but to her surprise, Daniel began walking towards her. Embarrassed,

| | |
|---|---|
| reluctantly | widerwillig |
| sympathy | Mitgefühl, Mitleid |

Emily started walking faster. She felt even more awkward when he called after her. She did not know him very well, and she could not think of any reason why he would want to start a conversation.

"Emily, wait," he called again. "Please, Emily."

Reluctantly, Emily stopped and turned around. When she saw the sadness in Daniel's eyes, she was surprised by the sympathy she felt towards him.

"I just wanted to know if you could possibly give Holly a message for me," Daniel continued. "I know she'll listen to you."

Emily's sympathetic expression disappeared in a second. This was exactly what Holly had asked her not to do.

"I'm afraid I can't do that," she replied without any emotion.

"Please," he repeated, but Emily was already walking away.

*ÜBUNG 24: Odd one out! Welches Wort ist das „schwarze Schaf"?*

1. homework, roller-skating, swimming, rock-climbing
2. oven, tray, wreath, dough
3. stocking, present, tinsel, bonfire
4. admire, neglect, avoid, reject
5. spicy, soppy, cinnamon, flavour

5

# An Unexpected Christmas Present

# 5

Trotz aller Ablenkungsversuche muss Holly immer noch dauernd an Daniel denken. Nacht für Nacht hat sie denselben Traum: Daniel versucht verzweifelt, ihr etwas zu sagen …
Gleichzeitig laufen die Vorbereitungen für den Weihnachtsmarkt weiter – der Stand der Freundinnen kommt super an! Aber dann steht dort plötzlich Daniel vor ihr und Holly ist viel zu verwirrt, um etwas zu sagen. Sie weiß einfach nicht mehr, was sie fühlt. Soll sie vielleicht doch versuchen, mit Daniel zu reden? Weihnachten hält mehr als eine Überraschung für sie bereit …

The Christmas market was just days away and the girls were busy preparing everything. They had bought all their ingredients, decided on their prices and asked Nina's parents to lend them some of their traditional decorations. Holly had even painted a sign saying "*Frohe Weihnachten*", which she had spelled wrong at first, to put at the top of their stall. Luckily, it had not been difficult to paint over the extra N that she had included, and now the sign looked perfect.
Holly put so much energy into the preparations for the market that she found there was not

| | |
|---|---|
| to lend sb. sth. | jmd. etw. leihen |
| snow globe | Schneekugel |
| hazy | verschwommen, unklar |
| to surge through | durchfluten, hereinbrechen über |
| to plead with sb. | jmd. anflehen |

much left for thinking about Daniel. But at the end of each day, once she had put her paintbrushes away and gone to bed, she could no longer control the thoughts that entered her head.

No matter how hard she tried to ignore memories of Daniel while she was awake, they came back to her at night. She had strange dreams that returned again and again to the same scene: white powder fell slowly around her as though she was in the centre of a giant snow globe. It fell so thickly that the landscape looked hazy and unreal. Suddenly she felt a snowball hit her from behind. She turned around and saw Daniel smiling at her. For a moment she felt so happy to see him that she wanted nothing more than to run up to him, to melt into his kiss and stay there forever. And then she remembered Ivy. Anger surged through her as she picked up as much snow as she could and threw it at him hard. She hit him again and again and ran away with tears in her eyes, trying not to look back. But she could not help turning around once. When she saw Daniel, his expression broke her heart in two. He was pleading with her to talk to him, calling her name. But she turned away and kept running. Finally she could no longer hear his shouts behind her and all that she could see was white.

Holly awoke abruptly. She had had the same dream five times that week. She felt angry, but she also had a strange feeling that she could not ignore – she desperately wanted to know what Daniel had been trying to tell her. The last images from her dream kept playing over and over in her head. And if she closed her eyes again, she could still see Daniel's tragic, pleading face as clearly as if he was right in front of her. What did he want to say? She knew that her dream was not real, but somehow she could not get the question out of her head.

*ÜBUNG 25: Synonyms. Welche Wörter vom Kapitelanfang haben dieselbe Bedeutung wie die folgenden Begriffe?*

1. decorated ..............................
2. at last ..............................
3. suddenly ..............................
4. fuzzy ..............................
5. woke up ..............................
6. incorrect ..............................
7. begging ..............................

Holly got up quickly and tried to focus on the day ahead. Today was the day of the Christmas market. Luckily, that meant that she would have plenty to distract her from the strange images that still drifted around her mind. She hoped that her excited thoughts would finally push them all away.

School also offered other distractions. She found out plenty of gossip in her lessons, even though it sometimes got her into trouble with her teachers for talking in class.

| | |
|---|---|
| desperately | verzweifelt, unbedingt |
| distraction | Ablenkung |
| gossip | Klatsch, Tratsch |

"I can't believe Jo fancies Kieran!" she said to the others as they got their things ready at the end of school. "I can't imagine them as a couple at all!"
"Me neither," said Nina. "But Holly, did you bring everything for this evening? We need to go and get our stall ready in the sports hall as soon as possible."
"Of course I did," said Holly proudly.
They had prepared the food and drink the night before, so now the four of them took their bags of food, drink and decorations and began to set everything up. They decorated the stall with Holly's sign and all of the things that they had borrowed from Nina's parents. Soon

it looked just like something from a real German Christmas market. Holly stood back and admired the festive display of delicious food and drink, nutcrackers, and candles beneath the sign that she had painted. It looked magical.

| | |
|---|---|
| ↯ to fancy sb. | auf jmd. stehen |
| to set sth. up | etw. aufbauen |
| to serve | (be)dienen |

Not long after they had finished setting everything up, people began to arrive. Holly soon noticed that their stall was becoming very popular. All four girls were kept busy serving the many people who wanted to try the things that they had made.

*ÜBUNG 26: Choose the correct tense. Unterstreiche jeweils die richtige Zeitform!*

1. Holly has/had plenty to think about that night.
2. Nina asked Holly if she will bring/had brought the things they needed.
3. Holly could not/cannot believe that Jo fancied Kieran.
4. "I can't/couldn't imagine them as a couple at all," she said.
5. "I bring/I'll bring the *Punsch*, and you can bring the *Lebkuchen*."

Holly was so busy that she did not see Daniel coming towards them. She looked up to give a piece of *Stollen* to a girl she knew from her Spanish class, and suddenly he was there in front of her. Her heart began to beat so loudly that she was sure he would be able to hear it from where he was standing.

"Holly, can we talk?" he asked her. There was no reply, so he quietly continued, "I miss you."

Holly felt that she would not be able to speak even if she wanted to. Silence filled the space between them until it was too late for her to reply.

Daniel looked at the ground. "Happy Christmas," he said without looking at her, and walked away.

Suddenly Holly felt an arm around her shoulder.

"Well done, Hol," Evie said firmly. "He deserves to see that you don't care about him anymore. Are you okay?"

Holly still felt too shaken to reply.

"You handled that really well," Nina added.

Holly did not understand their comments: she had done nothing. She had made no decision to remain silent, to punish Daniel or ignore him. She had simply been frozen by the strength of her feelings when she saw his face in front of her. She was shocked by the shape those feelings had taken: the emotion she felt was not anger or sadness, but love. But how could she still love Daniel after what he had done to her? It made no sense.

Holly could not understand what had just happened. She tried to pretend that things were just the same as before and continued serving people and eating a few of the delicious cakes and biscuits herself.

| | |
|---|---|
| shaken | erschüttert, aufgewühlt |
| to handle sth. | mit etw. umgehen |
| crumb | Krümel |
| She could not begin to explain it. | Sie konnte es nicht mal ansatzweise erklären. |
| ϟ to turn up | erscheinen, auftauchen |

Their stall was almost empty by nine o'clock, when the market closed. All that was left of the food was a few crumbs. Emily quickly counted up the money that they had made.

"Wow, a hundred and fifty pounds!" she said. "Fantastic!"

"We'll be able to buy each other some brilliant presents this year!" Evie added.

"But how are you, Holly?" Emily asked kindly. "That must have been difficult for you earlier. Are you okay?"

"Yeah, I'm fine," said Holly, yet somehow the words seemed false. She did not tell them how she was really feeling. She could not begin to explain it.

The days passed by until a single door remained unopened on Holly's Advent calendar. It was the day before Christmas Eve, and Holly's family were beginning to arrive for Christmas. Her uncle and aunt were the first to turn up, followed by her grandmother, and finally another uncle and her three cousins. Holly's older sister, Sophie, had also come back from university for the holidays a few days before, so the family was complete. The nights became long and were filled with talk until the early hours. Holly spent the days watching television, listening to all of Sophie's university gossip and playing computer games with her cousins. Surrounded by the people that she loved, Holly finally began to enjoy the festive mood that had been so slow to hit her this year.

*ÜBUNG 27: Who said what? Ordne die Aussagen den Sprechern zu!*

1. ❑ Emily said...
2. ❑ Evie added, ...
3. ❑ Nina told Holly...
4. ❑ Daniel asked, ...
5. ❑ Holly told the others...
6. ❑ Emily asked Holly, ...

a) "We'll be able to buy each other some brilliant presents this year!"
b) "But how are you, Holly?"
c) that they had made a hundred and fifty pounds.
d) that she had handled the situation well.
e) "Holly, can we talk?"
f) that she was fine, but the words seemed false.

| | |
|---|---|
| the early hours | nach Mitternacht |
| wide awake | hellwach |

Christmas Eve came and went. Holly did not have any special Christmas Eve traditions, but that day she thought of Nina and her family. She closed her eyes and imagined them opening their presents and looking at their Christmas tree for the first time. The thought made her feel warm inside.

Holly always found it difficult to sleep on the night before Christmas, but this year she had more on her mind than just presents. She tried breathing deeply and moving around into every position she could think of, but nothing she did helped her to drift off to sleep.

It was almost midnight, and Holly was lying at the wrong end of her bed with her eyes wide open. Suddenly, her phone made a sound. It was a message from Emily:

> R u awake? Can't sleep, too excited!
> Em x

Holly sat up at once, happy to be distracted from her thoughts. She called Emily, who took almost no time to answer.

"Can't sleep either, then?" Emily said brightly.

Clearly, she too was still wide awake in spite of the late hour. "Are you excited about tomorrow?"

"Well... yeah, I guess," Holly began, and then realized immediately that she was going to tell the truth.

"...But mainly I just can't stop thinking about Dan. I don't know what's wrong with me!"

Emily thought for a little while before speaking.

| | |
|---|---|
| gasp | Keuchen |
| to weigh up | abwägen |
| to move on | *hier:* etw. hinter sich lassen |

"I don't understand," she finally said. "Aren't you angry at him anymore for what he did?"

"Yes. No... I don't know how I feel," Holly replied. "It's strange. I can't forgive him for cheating on me, but when I saw him at the Christmas market, I.... You'll think I'm crazy..."

Holly did not finish the sentence and Emily was left wondering what she was trying to say.

"I'm sure I won't think that," Emily responded.

"You can tell me anything, Hol."

"I think I still love him," Holly said quietly.

From the other end of the phone line, Holly thought she heard a little gasp.

"Do you want to get back together?" Emily asked quickly.

"I couldn't do that. It would be impossible for me to trust him ever again. And anyway, he's with Ivy now. We've all seen them together."

Holly sighed. "Why am I even thinking about this?!"

Emily wished that she knew what to say. She had been expecting a conversation about Christmas presents, not a difficult problem. She simply could not imagine how to solve this. But then she remembered something. She knew from experience that it was possible to see one thing but to believe that you had seen something else.

"Holly," she said. "I know this might sound a bit stupid, but are you absolutely sure that Dan is going out with Ivy?"
"What do you mean?" asked Holly.
"Well, have you spoken to him since you broke up?"
"No, but I don't need to," Holly replied. Her voice suddenly sounded hard. "He's already made it very clear how he feels."
Emily thought for a moment. She seemed to be weighing up her words carefully. Finally, she continued.
"I don't know... maybe you should speak to him at least one last time. Otherwise, even if you're completely right about everything, you'll never know for sure. You haven't given him a chance to explain, so you'll never feel like you can move on."
"But I know what happened," Holly responded. "What is there to talk about?"
"I'm not sure. But sometimes things can be different to what they seem. Perhaps there's more to it."
"Maybe you're right," Holly said. "But I just can't see him again at the moment. I wouldn't even be able to speak to him – it's too painful."
"It's okay, don't worry about it now – but do try and get some sleep, yeah? And have a brilliant Christmas tomorrow."
"You too, Em. Thanks so much for being there for me."
"Anytime. Goodnight, Hol."
Holly put down the phone. What her friend had said had given her a lot to think about. But somehow she had to put it to the back of her mind, or she would never be able to sleep.

*ÜBUNG 28: Multiple choice. Kreuze jeweils die richtige Variante an!*

1. Holly could not...
   a) ❑ hide
   b) ❑ cover
   her feelings any longer.

2. Emily was not...
   a) ❑ clear
   b) ❑ sure
   that everything was as it seemed.

3. Emily said that Holly should speak to Dan...
   a) ❑ more than
   b) ❑ at least
   one more time.

4. Holly had a lot of things...
   a) ❑ on
   b) ❑ inside
   her mind.

5. Neither of the two friends had been able to...
   a) ❑ drop
   b) ❑ fall
   asleep yet.

6. Emily had expected a...
   a) ❑ conversation
   b) ❑ conservation
   about Christmas presents.

The next day, Holly was woken up by her youngest cousin, Ben. He could not wait any longer to open his presents, but had been told that he could not do so until everybody else was awake.
"Get up, Holly! Father Christmas has been!"
Ben was shouting in Holly's ear and pulling as hard as he could on her arm to get her out of bed.
Holly had stopped believing in Father Christmas many years ago, but she had still put her empty stocking at the end of the bed the night before, just like her young cousin. Now, through half-open eyes, she saw that it was full. There were so many presents inside that they spilled out onto the floor.

| | |
|---|---|
| drowsily | schläfrig |
| to be littered with | übersät sein mit |
| wrapping paper | Geschenk-papier |
| pile | Stapel |

She opened her stocking drowsily. As always, there was chocolate money, an orange and some nuts inside, as well as some small toys, games and a DVD of one of her favourite films.
Once the whole family was ready, they could also open their other Christmas presents, which had been gathering underneath the tree ever since the start of December. It took a long time to open them, and soon the floor of the living room was littered with wrapping paper. Holly wished that she could focus on the happy scene, but her mind was elsewhere.
Finally, there was nothing left beneath the tree, and opened presents sat in piles beside every family member. Holly's

pile included new clothes, jewellery, CDs and books – everything that she had wanted. Her mum and aunt had already left the room to start cooking Christmas dinner, and the rest of the family were relaxing around the television.

| | |
|---|---|
| roast turkey | gebratener Truthahn |
| parsnip | Pastinake |
| stuffing | Füllung |
| speech | Rede, Ansprache |
| locket | Medaillon |

Their Christmas dinner of roast turkey with potatoes, parsnips and stuffing was served at two o'clock. At around the same time, most of the country was sitting down to eat exactly the same meal. Many would also gather around the television a little later to watch the Queen's Christmas speech, but Holly's family did not. Instead, by five o'clock, they were all playing charades in the living room, when suddenly the sound of the doorbell interrupted the game.

"I'll get it," said Holly. She opened the door, but there was nobody on the other side. She could hear footsteps disappearing into the distance; all that was left by the door was a present and a card. She felt her heart beat faster when she saw her own name written in large letters on the envelope. She picked up the gift and the card before closing the door on the cold, dark evening outside.

She opened the present first. The silver wrapping paper fell away to reveal a box, which held a necklace with a beautiful golden locket. She slowly opened the locket and saw the miniature smiles of herself and Daniel stare up from the tiny photograph inside: it was the picture that Daniel had taken of them lying in the snow. She had not seen it since that day. A feeling of love and incredible sadness surged through her whole body. It was so strong that it felt like physical pain. Instinctively, she put her hand to her heart, where the pain was deepest. It took her a little while to open the card. She felt the envelope carefully with each finger, turning it around in her hands. She was not sure if she was ready to read what was inside. Eventually, she could not stop herself from tearing the envelope open and searching for the words that he had written to her:

| | |
|---|---|
| incredible | unglaublich |
| physical | körperlich |
| to run out of hope | die Hoffnung verlieren |

Dear Holly,

I still don't understand what has happened to us. I love you so much, even after everything, and I can't work out how to carry on like this. Please speak to me. I miss you more than I can begin to describe.
I hope you like the present – I don't know anything about jewellery, so I asked Ivy to help me find you something special in town. Then suddenly everything fell apart and I never had the chance to give it to you. That feels like so long ago now. I've kept this necklace ever since then, but now I'm running out of hope for us. So here it is – my Christmas present to you.

Love, Dan

Holly did not even think before flying down the street. Although she was wearing only a T-shirt and jeans, and just socks on her feet, she was not even aware of the cold. The only thing on her mind was the dark figure turning towards a nearby house that she had visited many times in the past.

*ÜBUNG 29: Put the events in order. Bringe die Sätze in die richtige Reihenfolge!*

a) Holly's family open their Christmas presents.
b) Holly reads the card that Dan wrote to her.
c) Holly's family play charades.
d) Holly's mum and aunt prepare the Christmas dinner.
e) Holly finds a present and a card by the door.
f) The doorbell rings.
g) Ben wakes Holly so that he can open his stocking.

| 1 | 2 | 3 | 4 | 5 | 6 | 7 |
|---|---|---|---|---|---|---|
| g | | | | | | |

"Wait!" she cried out to the person at the door of the house. "Wait, Dan!"

Daniel turned around, and she saw his face in the reflection of the Christmas tree lights inside. She ran towards him instinctively.

| | |
|---|---|
| to be aware of sth. | sich einer Sache bewusst sein |
| figure | Gestalt |
| sb.'s jaw drops | jmd. fällt die Kinnlade herunter |

"Is it true?" she asked. "You were just buying me a present that day when you went to town with Ivy?"

"Of course," replied Daniel. "I wanted to make sure I got you the right thing, so I asked for Ivy's help. I don't understand – what did you think I was doing?"

"I... I thought you were cheating on me with her," Holly said very quietly. Tears were pouring down her cheeks. "I heard Ivy talking in the bathroom about kissing you earlier that day."

"What?" asked Daniel, confusion written across his face.

"Yeah, she said you were the best kisser ever or something. And she called you a stupid nickname, uh... Danny, I think."

Daniel's jaw dropped.

"No, you idiot," he said.

He began to hug her and kiss her forehead, and looked like he might begin crying himself.

"Danny is Ivy's boyfriend in London. I can't believe you could have thought that about me."

| | |
|---|---|
| to sob | schluchzen |
| incoherently | unzusammenhängend |
| to swallow | schlucken |
| locked together | *hier:* ineinander verschlungen |
| to flutter | *hier:* rieseln |

Daniel turned away from her and held his head in his hands for a moment.

Holly immediately began to cry so much that she thought her wet face might freeze over in the bitter December cold. She had never felt more stupid in her whole life. She held Daniel from behind, sobbing onto his shoulder. She told him how sorry she was again and again, but the words fell out of her mouth incoherently.

Finally, Daniel turned back to her, held her tightly in his arms and said that he forgave her.

“It doesn’t matter anymore, Hol. We can finally be together again. I’ve missed you so much… I’ve dreamt about you every night.”

Holly looked up suddenly and swallowed her sobs.

“Me too,” she said. “Oh Dan, we really were made for each other.”

She held his face and stared into his beautiful eyes.

“I’m never letting you go again,” she said.

Holly and Daniel stood locked together beneath a thousand stars. Their faces were so close that she could feel his warm breath on her cheek. Nothing else seemed to matter besides the two of them. Even as tiny flakes of snow began to flutter down from the night sky, Holly did not notice the cold at all.

## *ÜBUNG 30: Made for each other? Seid ihr für einander geschaffen?*

1. How do you feel when you are with your boyfriend or crush?
   a) ❑ I feel like the luckiest person in the world. *(10 points)*
   b) ❑ I feel happy, even though it isn't always perfect. *(5 points)*
   c) ❑ Often I would rather be somewhere else. *(0 points)*

2. Do you find him easy to talk to?
   a) ❑ Very – we finish each other's sentences. *(10 points)*
   b) ❑ Quite easy because we have a lot in common. *(5 points)*
   c) ❑ Not really. Our conversations can be awkward at times. *(1 point)*

3. Can you trust your boyfriend?
   a) ❑ Yes. He is always there for me and would never hurt me. *(10 points)*
   b) ❑ Yes, I'm pretty sure I can trust him. *(5 points)*
   c) ❑ Maybe – but I don't know whether he should trust me! *(0 points)*

Your score: ……………

Daniel suddenly pulled Holly towards him and kissed her fiercely, with a passion that ran through her own body like electricity. It was as though the kiss had been building up for all of the weeks they had been apart and could not wait a moment longer to be set free. Holly had never been kissed like that in all her life. Even when Daniel pulled away, she felt like she was still tingling inside. She pulled him back into her arms and kissed him again with just as much passion.

| | |
|---|---|
| fiercely | wild, heftig |
| to be set free | freigelassen werden |
| to tingle | prickeln, kribbeln |
| to be drawn to | hingezogen werden zu |
| Portuguese | portugiesisch |
| butterfly | Schmetterling |

Suddenly, the front door flew open and Daniel's family spilled out into the garden excitedly. The children were all pointing at the snow that was now falling more thickly. But a moment later, their eyes were drawn to a different scene.

Holly turned around and saw the family looking at the two of them. The children were now staring with their hands over their mouths. Nobody said a word. Embarrassed, Holly immediately stepped away from Daniel.

"Holly!" cried Daniel's mother happily. "*Feliz Natal!*"

"That means merry Christmas in Portuguese," Daniel told Holly in a whisper.

His mum, who had always got on very well with Holly, ran over to give her a warm hug. Holly smiled and let go of her worries about what Daniel's family must think of her.

"Come inside, quickly! You must be cold," said Daniel's mum. Holly and Dan walked into the house together and sat down beside a Christmas tree covered in brightly coloured butterflies. Holly rested her head on Daniel's shoulder and held his hand tightly in hers. She was still holding the present and card in her other hand.

"Thank you for my locket," she said, a little shyly.

She still felt bad about everything that had happened.

"Here, I'll help you put it on," Daniel said. The look in his eyes told her once and for all that she had been forgiven. He opened the box and gently held the necklace up around Holly's neck before fastening it for her.

Holly's heart felt as light as air and so full of love that it was hard for her to believe that such a feeling could be real. Was this truly not one of her daydreams? She had to pinch herself to make sure.

She looked down at the golden locket that hung, shimmering, around her neck. It was beautiful. But that Christmas she had been given something even better. She had been given a kiss while tiny snowflakes fell from above, a kiss which restored the relationship she had thought was ruined forever.

| | |
|---|---|
| once and for all | ein für alle Mal |
| to fasten sth. | etw. schließen, zumachen |
| to pinch oneself | sich zwicken |
| to restore | wiederherstellen |

Even Holly's vivid imagination could not have created a more perfect Christmas present.

# Lösungen und Glossar

# Lösungen

*ÜBUNG 1:*

| | | | | | | | | | | |
|---|---|---|---|---|---|---|---|---|---|---|
| X | A | P | Y | J | A | M | A | S | Y | L |
| B | S | P | A | H | R | E | T | B | U | P |
| V | N | A | W | E | S | P | D | S | E | G |
| E | O | M | N | I | C | O | A | T | J | I |
| N | W | T | O | N | F | W | B | E | Z | G |
| A | B | G | P | W | A | D | G | M | O | G |
| T | A | W | M | I | Z | E | V | R | F | L |
| S | L | I | P | P | E | R | S | I | J | E |
| H | L | U | B | E | X | U | C | H | O | Z |
| I | M | F | A | Z | L | K | I | X | S | A |
| K | J | E | M | W | I | N | D | O | W | U |

Horizontal: pyjamas, coat, slippers, window
Vertikal: snowball, yawn, wipe, powder, giggle

*ÜBUNG 2:*

1. richtig 2. richtig 3. falsch 4. richtig 5. falsch 6. falsch 7. richtig

*ÜBUNG 3:*

0–8 points: You should think again about how important your friends are to you. If you keep putting boys before them, you may soon not have many left.

9–16 points: You don't always put boys first, but perhaps you could still think a bit more about your friends' feelings. Make sure that they don't feel left out.

17 points or more: It seems like you put your friends first. This is a great attitude because while boys may come and go, the friendships you have now could last forever.

*ÜBUNG 4:*

1. from 2. in 3. through 4. about 5. to 6. in 7. in 8. up 9. at 10. into

*ÜBUNG 5:*

1. Guy Fawkes tried to kill the King of England by putting gunpowder underneath the Houses of Parliament.
2. He was burnt in a fire as punishment.
3. People today watch firework displays and burn models of Guy Fawkes on bonfires to remember him.
4. Holly was late because she was with her boyfriend and forgot all about the firework display.
5. Nina does not understand why the English celebrate that somebody tried to kill the king.
6. It is usually made of straw and wood, and is dressed in historical clothes.

*ÜBUNG 6:*

1. bonfire 2. ball 3. sparks 4. ice 5. slippers

*ÜBUNG 7:*

1. duller 2. more beautiful, most beautiful 3. romantic, more romantic 4. happy, happiest 5. better, best 6. bad, worst

*ÜBUNG 8:*

1. insulted 2. jealous 3. fumes 4. moved 5. dislikes 6. daydream

*ÜBUNG 9:*

1. about 2. away 3. missing 4. cleared 5. never 6. discuss

*ÜBUNG 10:*

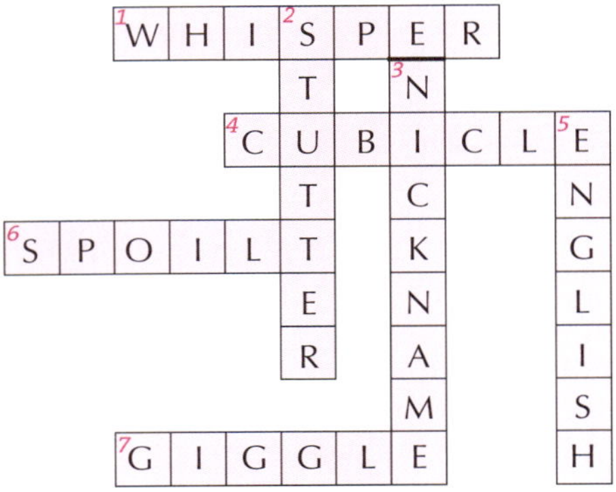


*ÜBUNG 11:*

1. Evie went to the bathroom to find Holly.
2. Holly tried to explain what had happened.
3. Evie comforted Holly.
4. Holly wanted to believe that what Evie said was the truth.
5. She had believed that Daniel would betray her.
6. Evie said, "Let me in!"

*ÜBUNG 12:*

1. froze – melted 2. nervously – confidently 3. silent – loud 4. beautiful – ugly 5. tight – loose 6. worse – better

*ÜBUNG 13:*

1. c 2. a 3. b 4. b 5. c

*ÜBUNG 14:*

1. He called me yesterday, too.
2. Holly lay down on her bed and stared at the ceiling.
3. I am not going to let him see how much he has upset me.
4. Holly told them to give Dan the cold shoulder.
5. I feel awful that I gave you the wrong advice yesterday.

*ÜBUNG 15:*

Mostly a): You and your friends don't seem to have important things in common, which could be a problem in the future. You need to look beyond how people look and how cool they are to find true friends.

Mostly b): It sounds like you have found a great group of friends, congratulations! With luck, you should stay friends forever.

Mostly c): There is a good chance that your friendships could last a long time. You care about your friends and will stay close to them as long as you continue making an effort.

*ÜBUNG 16:*

1. an 2. a 3. the 4. a 5. the 6. The 7. an

*ÜBUNG 17:*

1. couldn't 2. hadn't 3. wouldn't 4. can't 5. shouldn't, he's 6. You've

*ÜBUNG 18:*

| 1 | 2 | 3 | 4 | 5 | 6 | 7 |
|---|---|---|---|---|---|---|
| *b* | *f* | *e* | *g* | *d* | *a* | *c* |

*ÜBUNG 19:*

1. Holly's mum came and put her hand on her daughter's shoulder.
2. She offered Holly a mince pie.
3. Holly refused because she was on a diet.
4. Holly's mum told her she did not need to be on a diet.
5. Holly's mum decided to cheer Holly up with an early Christmas present.

*ÜBUNG 20:*

1. falsch 2. falsch 3. falsch 4. richtig 5. falsch 6. richtig 7. falsch

*ÜBUNG 21:*

1. Christmas Eve 2. coal 3. ingredients 4. kits 5. festive 6. trust

Lösung: market

*ÜBUNG 22:*

Mostly a): Traditions are important to you and you like to celebrate special events in a traditional way. This means that you have a lot to look forward to throughout the year – and plenty of parties to go to!

Mostly b): You aren't a traditional person at all. You don't believe that you have to do something a certain way just because other people do. This makes you independent and confident, and there is no reason to change.

Mostly c): You aren't particularly traditional, but you don't break traditions for no reason either. You respect that traditions are important to others and enjoy celebrating with friends and family.

*ÜBUNG 23:*

1. Holly spilled flour, eggshells and cinnamon on the floor.
2. The girls burned the first tray of biscuits by accident.
3. They were careful not to leave the second tray in the oven for too long.
4. Nina put the leftover food into a box to show to Mrs Skelton on Monday morning.
5. First the kitchen smelled of fruit and cinnamon, but then it filled with a burnt smell.
6. Holly promised herself that she would never again forget how important her friends were.

*ÜBUNG 24:*

1. homework 2. wreath 3. bonfire 4. admire 5. soppy

*ÜBUNG 25:*

1. adorned 2. finally 4. abruptly 4. hazy 5. awoke
6. wrong 7. pleading

*ÜBUNG 26:*

1. had 2. had brought 3. could not 4. can't 5. I'll bring

*ÜBUNG 27:*

1. c 2. a 3. d 4. e 5. f 6. b

*ÜBUNG 28:*

1. a 2. b 3. b 4. a 5. b 6. a

*ÜBUNG 29:*

| 1 | 2 | 3 | 4 | 5 | 6 | 7 |
|---|---|---|---|---|---|---|
| *g* | *a* | *d* | *c* | *f* | *e* | *b* |

*ÜBUNG 30:*

0 – 9 points: Bad news – you and your boyfriend or crush might not be right for each other. Make sure that he does not think you are more serious about the relationship than you really are.

10 – 20 points: Your relationship isn't perfect, but with time it could be something special. Wait and see what happens before giving your heart away.

21 points or more: It looks like you have a really special relationship. Make sure that he knows how you feel about him, and that he feels the same way, too!

# Glossar

| | |
|---|---|
| absentmindedly | geistesabwesend |
| to adjust (to) | sich gewöhnen an, sich anpassen |
| to admire | bewundern |
| Advent wreath | Adventskranz |
| to advise | (be)raten |
| to aim | zielen |
| all of a sudden | ganz plötzlich |
| apology | Entschuldigung |
| at once | *hier:* zugleich |
| to avoid | (ver)meiden |
| awkward | unangenehm |
| barely | kaum |
| to bear (bore, borne) sth. | etw. ertragen |
| to be aware of sth. | sich einer Sache bewusst sein |
| to be cancelled | gestrichen sein |
| to become (became, become) a blur | verschwimmen |
| to be drawn to | hingezogen werden zu |
| to be drowned out | übertönt werden |
| to be littered with | übersät sein mit |
| to be set free | freigelassen werden |
| to bet (bet, bet) | wetten |
| to betray sb. | jmd. betrügen |
| to be used to sth. | etw. gewohnt sein |
| blank | ausdruckslos |
| to blow one's nose | sich die Nase putzen |
| bonfire | Scheiterhaufen, großes Lagerfeuer |

| | |
|---|---|
| Bonfire Night | Die Nacht des 5. November, zur Erinnerung an den 1605 gescheiterten Plan, das Parlament zu sprengen |
| to bounce with excitement | vor Aufregung hüpfen |
| branch | Zweig |
| break-up | Trennung |
| bulge | Wölbung |
| to bump into sb. | mit jmd. zusammenstoßen |
| buried | *hier:* verschneit |
| to burst into tears | in Tränen ausbrechen |
| butterfly | Schmetterling |
| candlelit dinner | Abendessen bei Kerzenschein |
| carelessly | achtlos |
| celebration | Feier |
| changing room | Umkleidekabine |
| to chat | plaudern |
| to cheat (on sb.) | jmd. betrügen |
| cheek | Wange |
| cheerful | fröhlich |
| chest | Brust |
| Christmas Day | erster Weihnachtsfeiertag |
| Christmas Eve | Heiligabend |
| cinnamon | Zimt |
| classmate | Klassenkamerad(in) |
| to clear one's throat | sich räuspern |
| closely | *hier:* genau |
| coal | Kohle |
| to comfort sb. | jmd. trösten |
| confidence | Selbstbewusstsein |
| contest | Wettbewerb |
| ϟ country bumpkin | Landei |
| ϟ creep | Widerling |
| to cringe | zusammenzucken, erschaudern |
| crowd | (Menschen-)Menge |
| cruel | grausam, gemein |
| crumb | Krümel |

| | |
|---|---|
| crumpled | zerknittert |
| ϟ crush | Schwarm |
| cubicle | Kabine |
| to curl into a ball | sich zusammenrollen, sich einigeln |
| curly | lockig |
| defiantly | kämpferisch, trotzig |
| departure board | Abfahrtsanzeige |
| to deserve sth. | etw. verdient haben |
| desperately | verzweifelt, unbedingt |
| diary entry | Tagebucheintrag |
| disgusting | widerlich |
| distraction | Ablenkung |
| to distract sb. | jmd. ablenken |
| dizzy | schwindelig |
| dough | Teig |
| to dread sth. | große Angst haben vor |
| to drift | gleiten, ziehen |
| drowsily | schläfrig |
| dully | gedämpft, dumpf |
| to earn sb.'s trust | jmd.s Vertrauen gewinnen |
| to echo sth. | etw. wiederholen |
| elf | Elfe |
| embarrassed | verlegen, peinlich |
| encouragingly | ermutigend |
| eventually | schließlich |
| exaggerated | übertrieben |
| excitement | Aufregung, Freude |
| to exclaim | ausrufen |
| to fall (fell, fallen) apart | in die Brüche gehen |
| ϟ to fancy sb. | auf jmd. stehen |
| to fasten sth. | etw. schließen, zumachen |
| Father Christmas | Weihnachtsmann |
| to feel (felt, felt) insulted | beleidigt sein |
| festive | festlich, weihnachtlich |
| fiercely | wild, heftig |
| figure | Gestalt |

| | |
|---|---|
| firework display | Feuerwerk |
| fireworks | Feuerwerk(skörper) |
| flash | Aufleuchten, Lichtblitz |
| to flash | aufleuchten, blinken |
| flatly | *hier:* ausdruckslos |
| to flaunt sth. | etw. zur Schau stellen, protzen |
| flavour | Sorte, Geschmacksrichtung |
| flicker | Anflug, Schimmer |
| to flick one's hair | die Haare nach hinten werfen |
| fluffy | flauschig |
| to flutter | *hier:* rieseln |
| to focus on | sich konzentrieren auf |
| food for thought | Stoff zum Nachdenken |
| form tutor | Klassenlehrer(in) |
| to freeze (froze, frozen) | *hier:* erstarren |
| to fume | schäumen (vor Wut) |
| fuzzy | unklar, verschwommen |
| gasp | Keuchen |
| to gather | sich versammeln |
| gaudy | knallbunt |
| to get one's priorities right | seine Prioritäten (richtig) setzen |
| giant | riesig |
| to giggle | kichern |
| ϟ to give sb. the cold shoulder | jmd. die kalte Schulter zeigen |
| to glare | starren |
| glossy | glänzend |
| to glow | strahlen, scheinen |
| ϟ to go (all) soppy on sb. | rührselig werden |
| to go on a diet | eine Diät machen |
| gossip | Klatsch, Tratsch |
| gratefully | dankbar |
| grin | Grinsen |
| gunpowder | Schießpulver |
| hairdresser's | Friseur(laden) |
| to handle sth. | mit etw. umgehen |
| hazy | verschwommen, unklar |

| | |
|---|---|
| hint | Spur, Andeutung |
| to hiss | fauchen, zischen |
| horrible | schrecklich |
| Houses of Parliament | Parlamentsgebäude in London |
| how dare | wie kann es … wagen |
| hug | Umarmung |
| imaginary | imaginär, vorgestellt |
| to imagine sth. | sich etw. vorstellen (können) |
| to imitate | nachahmen |
| incoherently | unzusammenhängend |
| incredible | unglaublich |
| ingredients | Zutaten |
| innocent pose | Unschuldsgeste |
| to interrupt | unterbrechen |
| in time | *hier:* im Takt, im Rhythmus |
| jealous | eifersüchtig |
| jealousy | Eifersucht |
| to join in | mitmachen |
| to join sb. | sich zu jmd. gesellen |
| to jump to conclusions | voreilige Schlüsse ziehen |
| keypad | Tastenfeld |
| ϟ kit | Klamotten |
| lamely | lahm, schwach |
| to lend (lent, lent) sb. sth. | jmd. etw. leihen |
| let alone | geschweige denn |
| to line | säumen (Straße) |
| to live out sth. | etw. verwirklichen, ausleben |
| locked together | *hier:* ineinander verschlungen |
| locket | Medaillon |
| lopsidedly | schief, ungleich |
| to make it up to sb. | bei jmd. etw. wiedergutmachen |
| to melt | sich auflösen, schmelzen |
| merry | fröhlich, vergnügt |
| might as well | könnte ebenso gut |
| mince pie | Kuchen mit einer Füllung aus Dörrobst und Sirup |

| | |
|---|---|
| to mingle | sich vermischen |
| mischievous | verschmitzt |
| to move on | *hier:* etw. hinter sich lassen |
| muffled | gedämpft, leise |
| to neglect | vernachlässigen |
| news presenter | Nachrichtensprecher(in) |
| nutcracker | Nussknacker |
| on silent | auf lautlos |
| once and for all | ein für alle Mal |
| out of the question | ausgeschlossen |
| oven | Ofen |
| parsnip | Pastinake |
| passion | Leidenschaft |
| pastry | Gebäck |
| pattern | Muster |
| photosynthesis | Fotosynthese |
| physical | körperlich |
| pile | Stapel |
| to pinch oneself | sich zwicken |
| play | *hier:* Theaterstück |
| to plead with sb. | jmd. anflehen |
| Poison Ivy | *hier:* die giftige Ivy (wörtlich: Giftefeu) |
| to polish | polieren, putzen |
| Poor him! | Der Arme! |
| Portuguese | portugiesisch |
| ϟ posh | vornehm, piekfein |
| to pound | pochen, schlagen |
| to pour down | herabfließen |
| powder | Pulver, Puder |
| to pretend | vormachen, vorgeben |
| to promise | versprechen |
| to punch | *hier:* eintippen |
| to punish | bestrafen |
| quilt | Bettdecke |
| raw | *hier:* empfindlich, blank |
| recipe | Kochrezept |

| | |
|---|---|
| to refuse | sich weigern, ablehnen |
| to reject sth. | etw. ablehnen |
| reliable | zuverlässig |
| relieved | erleichtert |
| reluctantly | widerwillig |
| reminder | Andenken, Erinnerung |
| to restore | wiederherstellen |
| roast turkey | gebratener Truthahn |
| routine | *hier:* Alltag |
| ruined | zerstört, ruiniert |
| to run out of hope | die Hoffnung verlieren |
| sb.'s heart sinks | jmd. wird das Herz schwer |
| sb.'s jaw drops | jmd. fällt die Kinnlade herunter |
| scene | Aussicht, Szenerie |
| screen | Bildschirm |
| sculpture | Skulptur |
| sense of direction | Orientierungssinn |
| sensitive | verständnisvoll, sensibel |
| to serve | (be)dienen |
| to set (set, set) sth. up | etw. aufbauen |
| shaken | erschüttert, aufgewühlt |
| to shatter | zerstören |
| She could not begin to explain it. | Sie konnte es nicht mal ansatzweise erklären. |
| to shimmer | schimmern, schillern |
| to shudder | zittern, erschaudern |
| sickening | ekelhaft, unerträglich |
| to sigh | seufzen |
| to silence | zum Schweigen bringen |
| slippers | Hausschuhe |
| smudge | Schmierfleck |
| to snap | *hier:* hochschrecken |
| to sniff | schniefen |
| snow globe | Schneekugel |
| sob | Schluchzer |
| to sob | schluchzen |

| | |
|---|---|
| soothingly | besänftigend |
| spark | Funke |
| sparkler | Wunderkerze |
| speech | Rede, Ansprache |
| spicy | würzig |
| to spill | strömen; verschütten |
| spoilt | verzogen, verwöhnt |
| stab of pain | stechender Schmerz |
| stall | Stand |
| to stand up for sb. | sich für jmd. einsetzen |
| to stare | starren |
| stocking | Strumpf |
| straw | Stroh |
| stubbornly | hartnäckig |
| to stuff | stopfen |
| stuffing | Füllung |
| to stutter | stottern |
| sudden | plötzlich |
| to suggest | vorschlagen |
| suit | Anzug |
| to support sb. | jmd. unterstützen |
| to suppose | denken, annehmen |
| sure enough | tatsächlich |
| to surge through | durchfluten, hereinbrechen über |
| to surrender | aufgeben, sich ergeben |
| to surround | umgeben |
| to swallow | schlucken |
| swirl | Gewirr |
| to swirl | wirbeln |
| switch | *hier:* Rute |
| sympathetically | verständnisvoll |
| sympathy | Mitgefühl, Mitleid |
| to tackle | angreifen (Fußball) |
| to take sb.'s mind off sth. | jmd. von etw. ablenken |
| target | Ziel |
| to tear (tore, torn) | (zer)reißen |

| | |
|---|---|
| Tears welled up in her eyes. | Ihr stiegen Tränen in die Augen. |
| text (message) | SMS |
| That's fine by me. | Das passt mir gut. |
| the early hours | nach Mitternacht |
| there's no point in | es hat keinen Sinn (zu) |
| to tingle | prickeln, kribbeln |
| tinsel | Lametta, Flitter |
| tissue | (Papier-)Taschentuch |
| to torment | quälen |
| tray | *hier:* Backblech |
| to tremble | zittern |
| to trudge | trotten, latschen |
| to trust | vertrauen |
| ϟ to turn up | erscheinen, auftauchen |
| to twirl | sich drehen, wirbeln |
| to twist | (das Gesicht) verziehen |
| ϟ to two-time sb. | jmd. betrügen |
| understanding | verständnisvoll |
| uneasy | angespannt, unbehaglich |
| unmistakably | unverkennbar |
| unreasonable | unvernünftig |
| to upset (upset, upset) sb. | jmd. aufregen |
| vivid imagination | lebhafte Fantasie |
| to waft | wehen, tönen |
| to wail | heulen, jammern |
| to weigh up | abwägen |
| wellington boots | Gummistiefel |
| whisper | Flüstern |
| wide awake | hellwach |
| window display | Schaufensterauslage |
| to wipe | (ab)wischen |
| wrapping paper | Geschenkpapier |
| to yawn | gähnen |
| zip | Reißverschluss |